The Financial Troubleshooter

Spotting and Solving
Financial Problems
in Your Company

Joel G. Siegel

Jae K. Shim

David Minars

McGraw-Hill, Inc.

New York   San Francisco   Washington, D.C.   Auckland   Bogotá
Caracas   Lisbon   London   Madrid   Mexico City   Milan
Montreal   New Delhi   San Juan   Singapore
Sydney   Tokyo   Toronto

Library of Congress Cataloging-in-Publication Data

Siegel, Joel G.
    The financial troubleshooter : spotting and solving financial
  problems in your company / Joel G. Siegel, Jae K. Shim,
  David Minars.
        p.   cm.
    ISBN 0-07-057603-3 — ISBN 0-07-057604-1 (pbk.)
    1. Corporations—Finance.   I. Shim, Jae K.   II. Minars, David.
  III. Title.
  HG4026.S487   1993
  658.15—dc20   92-35026
                                                                    CIP

  2 3 4 5 6 7 8 9 0   DOC/DOC   9 8 7 6 5 4 3

ISBN   0-07-057603-3   {HC}
ISBN   0-07-057604-1   {PBK}

*The sponsoring editor for this book was Caroline Carney, the editing
supervisor was Ann Craig, and the production supervisor was Donald
F. Schmidt. It was set in Century Schoolbook by McGraw-Hill's
Professional Book Group composition unit.*

Printed and bound by R. R. Donnelley & Sons Company.

To

Roberta M. Siegel,
loving wife and colleague

Chung Shim,
loving and dedicated wife

Iris Minars,
my best partner and friend

Contents

Preface

A manager's success depends largely on his or her ability to manage a company's assets. This mission is complicated by the interdependent nature of a company's finances. One short-term financial problem, such as a cash flow shortage, can cause a longer-term credit problem, such as denials for bank loans. The successful manager must be able to quickly identify and resolve such short-term problems in order to prevent their long-term deleterious effects.

The Financial Troubleshooter is an indispensable handy desk reference for effective business managers. Covering every facet of the daily management of a business's finances, it is designed to help managers pinpoint, resolve, and prevent financial problems. In each case, it also points out potential spillover effects—the ways in which a problem in one sector can disrupt operations in other areas.

Inspired in part by the practical troubleshooting books written for car and home repair, *The Financial Troubleshooter* is a hands-on, action-oriented manual for business managers, accountants, marketing managers, financial managers and officers, credit managers, entrepreneurs, and all business professionals who have fiscal responsibilities. One of the book's strongest features is its user-friendly, uniform format. Each financial problem is illuminated in the following, step-by-step fashion:

1. Problem

2. Identifying Symptoms

3. Causes

4. Measurement and Analysis

5. Repair

6. Prevention Techniques

7. Spillover Effects

Spillover Effects, the final item covered under each problem, will be of particular value to managers seeking to prevent costly systemic disruptions. Cross-references throughout the book provide a running, in-text index of related areas.

Acknowledgments

We want to express our deep appreciation to Caroline Carney for her outstanding editorial assistance while we were writing this book. Her very professional work is much appreciated and respected. We thank her for a superb job!

We also acknowledge with great thanks Theodore Nardin, who gave us the idea and overall framework for *The Financial Troubleshooter*. The lead author has had the good fortune to have worked with Ted for many years on ten other books. He is a man of great intelligence, integrity, motivation, and dedication to his work.

Thanks also go to Gerald Lombardi, the developmental editor, for his contributions to the book's final form.

Joel G. Siegel
Jae K. Shim
David Minars

1

Cash Flow
Disruptions

Failure to keep track of money can doom a business. Without monitoring its cash—measuring it, investing it, borrowing it, and collecting it—an enterprise can wind up insolvent or bankrupt. Without proper cash flow, a company cannot pay its bills on time, which may injure its credit rating. Bankruptcies are caused by lack of cash as well as by lack of profits.

Having "enough" cash means having enough cash available *at the right time*. A situation that requires management to advise a lender, creditor, or the IRS that the company cannot pay indicates a lack of managerial competence and control. Methods must be found to accelerate cash inflows and delay cash outflows.

Problem: Inadequate Cash Position

IDENTIFYING SYMPTOM. Cash is unavailable to pay operating expenses as they become due to buy inventory, to pay debt, to meet dividends, or to support a company's expansion policies. A portion of the cash is restricted. (For example, a compensating balance does not represent "free" cash.)

CAUSES. The firm's day-to-day operations are not perfectly synchronized.

- Contractual obligations require that the firm retain a minimal balance at all times.

- The company is required to hold cash balances to compensate banks for services provided.

- Weak collection policies leave the firm showing a net income but lacking liquid funds. (You can go broke while making a profit.)

- Cash held in a politically unstable foreign country, in a time deposit, or in a temporary escrow account is not available.

MEASUREMENT AND ANALYSIS. Management must determine

the percentage of the cash balance that is unavailable for use. Liquidity is improved when earnings are backed up by cash. A declining cash flow from operations to net income indicates a cash flow problem.

Consider the following:

- Cash flow generated from operations before interest expense.

- Cash flow generated from operations less cash payments required to pay debt principal, dividends, and capital expenditures.

- Cash reinvestment ratio (cash employed/cash obtained). Cash employed equals increase in gross plant and equipment plus increase in net working capital. Cash obtained equals income after tax plus depreciation. A high cash reinvestment ratio indicates that more cash is being used in the business.

Examine the trend in the ratio of sales to cash. A high turnover rate points to cash inadequacy and may lead to financial problems if further financing is not available at reasonable rates.

Management must compute the following ratios:

- Cash from sales to total sales. A high ratio means that sales are generating cash flow. A high ratio also indicates quality sales dollars.

- Cash debt coverage equal to cash flow from operations less dividends divided by total debt. Cash flow from operations less dividends is referred to as retained operating cash flow and indicates the number of years current cash flows will be needed to pay debt. A high ratio shows that the company can repay debt.

- Cash flow from operations less dividends divided by the current maturities of long-term debt. This ratio can be adjusted further by adding to the denominator current liabilities or other fixed commitments, such as lease obligations.

- Cash dividend coverage equal to cash flow from operations divided by total dividends. This ratio reflects the company's ability to meet current dividends from operating cash flow.

- The capital acquisitions ratio equals cash flow from operations less dividends divided by cash paid for acquisitions. This ratio reveals the company's ability to finance capital expenditures from internal sources.

- Net cash flows for investing activities divided by net cash flows from financing activities compares the total funds needed for investment (purchase of fixed assets and investments in securities) to funds generated from financing (debt and equity issuances). The issue is whether the fund sources are adequate to meet investment requirements.

- Net cash flows for investing divided by net cash flows from operating and financing activities compares the funds needed for investment to the funds obtained from financing and operations.

- Cash return on assets equals cash flow from operations before interest and taxes divided by total assets. A higher ratio indicates a greater cash return earned on assets employed. However, this ratio contains no provision for replacing assets or for future commitments.

- Cash flow from operations divided by total debt plus stockholders' equity indicates the internal generation of cash available to creditors and investors.

- Cash flow from operations divided by stockholders' equity indicates the return earned by stockholders.

REPAIR

- Obtain immediate financing by incurring debt or by issuing preferred or common shares to provide needed cash to operate effectively.

- Establish open lines of credit. (Perhaps refinancing may be made at lower interest rates.)

- Sell assets to generate cash.

- Enter into sales-leaseback arrangements.

- Postpone cash payments where possible.

- Rent rather than buy.

- Make only those cash payments necessary to maintain current operations.

- Reduce selling prices on products to generate cash flow.

PREVENTION TECHNIQUES

- Check new customers' credit standings by reviewing TRW and Dun and Bradstreet reports.

- Analyze cash collection and disbursement processes since these areas can be exploited to economize on cash holdings.

- Analyze customer payment history, such as average number of days beyond terms. Past due notices should be sent and phone calls made.

Policies should be designed to take advantage of the float in the payment and disbursement system. To speed cash collections, customers should be instructed to send their payments to the company's headquarters, or to a nearby collection center to minimize mail delay. Customers can also be instructed to mail payments to a post office box that is only a few hundred miles away. The post office box should be emptied several times a day. Large checks, for example, those over $1 million, should be picked up by courier service rather than having customers mail them. Customers who make the same purchases every month can give the seller a preauthorized check (PAC) that allows the payee (the company owed the money) to write a check on the payor's account and to deposit it at an agreed upon time. This procedure will eliminate the mail float. Companies should pay bills on time, not before or after they are due. Set up checking accounts in areas located a long distance from suppliers. This will increase the time it takes for a check to clear the banking system for eventual payment. Large cash payments to a selling company can be made by wire transfers or through an automated clearinghouse. This will give the vendor faster access to the cash proceeds.

- Improve credit and collection policies to customers. Cash sales should be encouraged. Credit sales must require a significant down payment and short payment terms. Delinquent balances should be charged interest.

- Extend the maturity dates on debt to retain cash longer.

- Prepare cash forecasts to improve financial planning. The forecasts will help to highlight problem times when the cash position will be weak.

- Engage in joint ventures where the other company provides the cash funding.

- Minimize restrictions on cash.

SPILLOVER EFFECTS.   If financing is available, the deficient cash position will require higher interest rates on loans and restrictions on the business. A company that is out of cash cannot operate effectively, resulting in declining liquidity, profitability, growth, and possible insolvency and bankruptcy.

See also CASH OUTFLOWS EXCEED CASH INFLOWS, DELAYED CUSTOMER PAYMENTS, GOING BROKE WHILE MAINTAINING PROFITS, INEFFICIENT USE OF CASH, and PAYING CASH TOO SOON.

Problem: Surplus Funds

IDENTIFYING SYMPTOM.   The funds in the cash account keep increasing, while current liabilities remain relatively unchanged.

CAUSE.   The cash generated from operations, investments, and financing is not being reinvested.

MEASUREMENT AND ANALYSIS. Short-term liquidity ratios can be used to determine whether surplus funds are excessive and nonproductive. Cash flow from operations to current liabilities is an effective ratio used to measure surplus funds. If the ratio keeps increasing, it can indicate that cash inflows are increasing and need to be invested. However, cash from investments and financing should also be taken into account.

REPAIR. Companies frequently accumulate cash balances that they do not require for their current needs or operations. This surplus cash can be invested in marketable securities, or used to reduce outstanding debt or increase compensating balances at banks. When investing excess funds, firms must weigh the safety of the security against its liquidity, maturity, and yield. A survey of cash managers based on the Fortune 1000 list of large industrial firms, indicated that Eurodollar CDs, commercial paper, domestic CDs, and repurchase agreements were the most popular vehicles for investing their short-term portfolios. Aggressive cash managers ranked *yield* first, *security* second, and *maturity* third. Moderate managers ranked *security* first, *yield* second, and *maturity* third.

PREVENTION TECHNIQUES

- Use surplus funds to enhance earnings.
- Develop a formal investment policy detailing sources of surplus funds, types of eligible investments, parameters of investment size and length, executives authorized to make investment decisions, transaction reporting requirements, and parties with whom transactions can be made.
- Pay debt on a regular basis from operating profits.

SPILLOVER EFFECTS. Having too much cash on hand can result in lost opportunities to earn a financial return. A company that does not use its cash efficiently can expect problems with financing, reduced growth, and lower profits.

See also INEFFICIENT USE OF CASH.

Problem: Delayed Customer Payments

IDENTIFYING SYMPTOMS

- Inability to collect an unusually high amount of accounts receivable.
- Customers paying later than usual and not in full.

CAUSES

- Clients are experiencing declining profitability and depressed economic conditions.
- The company's credit department is inexperienced and ineffective.

MEASUREMENT AND ANALYSIS.   The longer the collection period applicable to an account receivable, the higher the company's receivables investment and its cost of extending credit to its customers. The bad-debt ratio, which is the portion of accounts receivables that is never collected, is an overall measure of the possibility of incurring bad debts. The higher the company's ratio, the greater the cost of extending credit.

REPAIR

- Offer cash discounts to customers for early payment. This will speed up the collection of accounts receivable, and by extension, reduce the company's receivables investment and associated costs. Offsetting these savings is the cost of the discounts that are taken. Implement a discount policy only if the return on funds obtained from early collection is greater than the cost of the discount.

- Reduce the delay in receiving customer payments by:

    Sending notices or letters requesting payment of the past-due status of the account

    Telephoning or visiting the customer

    Employing a collection agency

    Taking legal action

- Refuse to make new shipments until all past-due receivables are paid.

- Include coded *return envelopes* or custom preaddressed, stamped envelopes with invoices.

- Send bills to customers when the order is shipped. The sooner a bill is received, the faster it will be paid.

- Correct invoice errors immediately, since the customer will not pay a bill until it is correct.

- Require deposits on large or custom orders, or bill as the work progresses.

- Set up a system to handle seasonal peak loads to avoid invoicing delays.

- Use COD terms for marginal customers.
- Charge interest on accounts receivable that are past due. If the customer has a financial problem, ask for a postdated check.
- Have funds electronically transferred (EFT) from customers. With EFT, a fund transfer is charged to the customer's bank account the same day it is credited to your bank account. As a result, payment *float* disappears, since funds are instantly available. It is a paperless transaction. Fewer receipts are lost or stolen.
- Use customer credit cards, which are automatically validated at the retail store.

PREVENTION TECHNIQUES. To enjoy the benefits of expeditious check clearance at low cost, institute a lockbox system. Under this system, regional collection offices (such as a post office box or private mail box) are set up. Customers are requested to forward their check to the post office box in their geographic region where a local bank picks up the checks for immediate deposit. The receiving bank remits to the company a list of checks received by account, a daily total, and any remittance documents. To speed up manual operations, there is a return document in the form of a paper or card which is read by an optimal character recognition device. It gives the business earlier notification of bad checks.

The corporation should determine the average dollar amount of checks received, cost of clerical operations eliminated, and reduction in "mail float" days. Because per-item processing cost is usually significant, a lockbox is most advantageous for low-volume, high-dollar collections. But the system is becoming increasingly available to small businesses with high-volume, low-dollar receipts as technological advances lower the per-item cost.

Cash may also be received faster from customers if they have given the company permission to routinely and automatically charge their accounts. This is referred to as *preauthorized* debits (PADs). PADs save a company the costs of processing invoices and payments. They also work well for repeated, constant charges at given time intervals.

Lastly, through the use of debit cards at an automatic teller machine (ATM), funds may be transferred electronically from the customer's account to the account of the small business.

SPILLOVER EFFECTS. A delay in cash payments from customers may create a cash flow problem because the company is not receiving the funds necessary to go on operating. The firm also loses a return on the delayed cash since it cannot invest the money. As a result, profitability will be adversely affected. Further, the company may need the funds to pay operating expenses and debt, purchase fixed assets, and take advantage of other opportunities that may arise. In an extreme case, if the company does not receive needed cash, it may risk insolvency and failure.

See also CASH OUTFLOWS EXCEED CASH INFLOWS, INEFFICIENT USE OF CASH, and INADEQUATE CASH POSITION.

Problem: Paying Cash Too Soon

IDENTIFYING SYMPTOMS

- Poor cash position
- Impaired credit rating
- Making full payments on accounts

CAUSES

- Poor cash management
- Improper cash analysis and poor decision making
- Lack of standard cash payment procedures
- Failure to use the most up-to-date cash planning and computer software and cash models

MEASUREMENT AND ANALYSIS.   The savings in delaying cash payment should be computed. The business may earn a return on the cash by holding it longer within the company.

Example: Every two weeks the company issues checks that average $500,000 and take three days to clear. The CFO wants to find out how much money can be saved annually if the transfer of funds is delayed from an interest-bearing account that pays 0.0384 percent per day (annual rate of 14 percent) for those three days.

$$\$500{,}000 \times (0.000384 \times 3) = \$576$$

The savings per year is $576 × 26 (yearly payrolls) = $14,976

Cash models should be used in cash management to minimize the sum of the fixed costs of transactions *and* the opportunity cost of holding cash balances.

REPAIR

- Never pay vendors early.
- Stretch payment dates to tolerant payers as long as no finance charge or impairment in credit results.
- Decide who should be paid first and who last.

- Deposit funds into checking and payroll accounts when checks are expected to clear. Many full-service banks offer customers consulting services pointing out structural defects in the Federal Reserve and other collection systems that allow a business to extend the payment period.
- Make partial payments and/or postdate checks.
- Request more information about an invoice before paying it.
- Mail payments late in the day or on Fridays.
- Use cash models for cash management.

PREVENTION TECHNIQUES

- Centralize the payables operation, so that debt may be paid at the most opportune time.
- Use payment drafts, in which payment is *not* made on demand. Instead, the draft is presented for collection to the bank, which in turn goes to the issuer to accept it. A draft may be used to allow for inspection before payment. When approved, the business deposits the funds. As a result, a smaller checking balance is required.
- Draw checks on remote banks.
- Mail from post offices with limited service or where mail has to go through numerous handling points. Checks can also be mailed from a location far removed from both the payee and drawee banks.
- Use probability analysis to determine the expected date for checks to clear.
- Use a charge account to lengthen the time between buying goods and paying for them.
- Avoid prepaid expenses.
- Compensate others with noncash consideration, such as stock or notes.
- Delay the frequency of payments to employees. Avoid giving them cash advances for travel and entertainment or loans. Have a monthly payroll rather than a weekly payroll. Ask employees to take furloughs (e.g., two weeks off without pay) or give up a current paycheck to be paid at a later date.
- Pay commissions on sales when the receivables are collected instead of when the sales are made.
- Engage in barter arrangements to avoid cash payments.
- Use cash flow software for day-to-day cash management, planning and analyzing cash flows, and determining payment dates.

SPILLOVER EFFECTS.   The result of paying early is less cash on hand, less liquidity, a lower rate of return earned, and possibly higher financing costs. This may result in cash problems and a decline in profits.

See also CASH OUTFLOWS EXCEED CASH INFLOWS, DELAYED CUSTOMER PAYMENTS, INEFFICIENT USE OF CASH, and INADEQUATE CASH POSITION.

Problem: Cash Outflows Exceed Cash Inflows

IDENTIFYING SYMPTOMS

- Declining profits
- Cash flow problems
- Increased use of credit lines
- Failure to pay bills or debt on time

CAUSES

- Slow collections from customers
- Low profit margin
- Paying bills before their due date
- Failure to expedite the collection of accounts receivable and reduce the lag between when customers pay their bills and when the checks are converted into cash
- Overspending
- Excessive debt
- Failure to fully assess a customer's credit risk

MEASUREMENT AND ANALYSIS.   To effectively control cash flows, management must understand the basic difference between accounting profits shown on the bottom line of the income statement and economic profits (*cash flows*).

REPAIR

- Speed up collections by offering discounts and relaxing credit standards. (But beware of creating more bad debts.)
- Stretch payables as long as possible.
- Sell off assets to reduce debt.

- Pay expenses and other obligations only at their due date.
- Buy used assets rather than new ones.

PREVENTION TECHNIQUES

- Establish a line of credit with banks.
- Try to manage receivables and spend more time on the efficient payment of accounts payable.
- Use cash management models that can help determine the optimal cash that a company should have available for operations. (*See* PAYING CASH TOO SOON for a full discussion of cash models.)

SPILLOVER EFFECTS.   When cash outflows exceed cash inflows, the borrower may have to finance its expansion at premium borrowing rates, thereby reducing profit margins. This often leads to sacrificing quality because the business can no longer afford extra staff or necessary expenditures. Inadequate cash flow will also result in lower credit ratings, decline in the market price of the issuing company's stocks and bonds, financial inability to make profitable investments at the right time, and, in severe cases, insolvency and bankruptcy.

See also DELAYED CUSTOMER PAYMENTS, GOING BROKE WHILE MAINTAINING PROFITS, INADEQUATE CASH POSITION, and INEFFICIENT USE OF CASH.

Problem: Going Broke While Maintaining Profits

IDENTIFYING SYMPTOMS

- The company shows a profit but has no cash.
- Management mistakes accounts receivable for cash, while daily payments are made for inventory purchases, payroll, and taxes.
- The company fails to budget properly for capital expenditures and emergencies.

CAUSES

- Failure to institute an effective cash management system
- Failure to develop a realistic business plan that estimates financial needs, identifies corporate strengths and weaknesses, and sets profit goals and policies
- Overspending and excessive debt

MEASUREMENT AND ANALYSIS. The company must develop a plan for cash inflows and outflows. The firm must also institute an effective cash collection policy.

REPAIR

- Study the cash flow cycle of the business.
- Prepare a monthly or quarterly cash budget forecast.
- Calculate current ratios to determine whether they are within the normal industry range.
- Bill credit sales promptly and maintain realistic credit policies.
- Use COD terms for chronic slow payers.

PREVENTION TECHNIQUES

- Establish both a lockbox system and regional offices for the rapid processing of checks that originate at distant points.
- Obtain working capital from suppliers of merchandise, materials, and equipment by making purchases from suppliers who do not demand immediate payment.
- Establish domestic letters of credit, whereby a bank makes a written commitment on behalf of a buyer to pay the seller for goods shipped.
- Lease an asset instead of purchasing it.
- Pay overtime or hire temporary help to reduce salaries and wages in a labor-intensive business.

SPILLOVER EFFECTS. If financing is available, a deficient cash position will require higher interest rates on loans and restrict business. A company that is out of cash cannot operate effectively and its profitability will decline. Management may face a net operating loss even if cash has increased during a given period.

See also CASH OUTFLOWS EXCEED CASH INFLOWS, DELAYED CUSTOMER PAYMENTS, and INADEQUATE CASH POSITION.

Problem: Inefficient Use of Cash

IDENTIFYING SYMPTOMS

- The company does not have enough cash to meet current debt obligations.

- There is more cash on hand than is necessary to cover operations, and this cash is not generating investment income.
- The profit margin is getting lower.

CAUSES

- Inefficient collection procedures
- Poor disbursement policies
- Inventory or capital asset overbuying
- Inefficient use of tax deferral techniques
- Overinvesting in short- or long-term assets

MEASUREMENT AND ANALYSIS.   A company's ability to sell inventory and collect receivables is fundamental to its success. A cash flow statement is the best tool for measuring cash inflows and outflows. It outlines cash flows from operating, investing, and financing activities and shows the net change in cash and cash equivalents during a given period.

Use comparative analysis to identify important ratios that reveal the correct collection period and the correct average inventory period for the business. (*See* INADEQUATE LIQUIDITY and INADEQUATE WORKING CAPITAL.) When studying these ratios, it is important to compare them to industry norms.

Example: Assume that a company developed the following data regarding average collection periods and average accounts receivable investments for two periods.

	Current	Prior
Average collection period (in days)	55	44
Average accounts receivable investment (per $1000 in daily sales)	$55,000	$44,000

Measured against the company's previous collection period, there is an 11-day increase in the average collection period. This produces an $11,000 decrease in the company's cash capability for each $1000 in daily sales. Management must also compare the company's collection period with that of a competitor.

REPAIR

- Avoid expensive overinvestment in fixed assets.
- Make a reliable cash forecast of projected inflows and outflows and of their timing.

- Use a zero balance account (ZBA) to speed up cash inflows and slow down cash outflows. In a ZBA, a master account is set up to receive all checks coming into the zero-balance system. As checks clear through the ZBA on which they are issued, funds are transferred to these accounts from the master account. Thus funds are transferred on a daily basis to cover the checks that have cleared, leaving a zero balance at the end of the day.
- Have customers mail their payments to nearby collection centers to minimize mail delay.

PREVENTION TECHNIQUES

- Use billing and collection procedures to reduce the time between shipping, invoicing, and second notices.
- Take advantage of vendors' discount policies for early payment.
- Use cash flow software to help prepare budgets and cash flow forecasts and time payables.
- Anticipate the total cash capability necessary for an investment in fixed assets.

SPILLOVER EFFECTS.   When cash outflows exceed cash inflows, a company may be unable to pay its debts as they become due. As a result, it can face strict loan terms from banks and stringent credit terms from vendors. The company's inability to pay cash dividends might affect the price of its stock and its ability to raise additional capital. A company that is subject to minimum cash availability cannot operate effectively, resulting in declining profitability and possible insolvency and bankruptcy.

See also CASH OUTFLOWS EXCEED CASH INFLOWS, DELAYED CUSTOMER PAYMENTS, INADEQUATE CASH POSITION, INADEQUATE LIQUIDITY, PAYING CASH TOO SOON, and SURPLUS FUNDS.

Disarray in Accounts Payable and Receivable

If suppliers' increased costs cannot be passed on to consumers in the form of higher prices, profit margins will shrink. Granting credit to risky customers will result in bad debt losses. On the other hand, excessively tight credit will lose both new and repeat business. Financial managers must always guard against fraudulent transactions.

Problem: Vendor's Price Increases

IDENTIFYING SYMPTOMS

- The vendor continually raises prices or raises them above the rate of inflation.
- The purchasing company cannot raise sales prices to absorb the increased cost of materials and services and still make a reasonable profit.

CAUSES

- A vendor must raise prices because the costs of its raw materials, labor costs, and overhead have also increased.
- A seller believes that its customers have to pay the increased charges because it enjoys a monopoly.
- A seller feels that its product has been underpriced and decides to charge what the changing market will absorb.

MEASUREMENT AND ANALYSIS

- The purchasing department has reported that the supplier is increasing costs with each purchase order.
- Actual costs exceed budgeted costs for the period under review.

- Total expenditures for this product are substantially higher than were total costs for the same period in the preceding year.

- Management has determined that it cannot continue to raise the cost of its product or service without incurring a loss of sales or a sales territory to competitors.

REPAIR

- Form a joint venture to manufacture the product or provide the service with another company that also has the same production requirements.

- Try to enter into a barter arrangement, trading your company's product or service in return for the seller's merchandise or services.

- If possible, purchase the supplier or find an alternative supplier.

- Offer to help another company develop the capacity to supply the goods or services that your company needs.

- Make the goods or produce the services yourself.

- Substitute another item or service in place of the current product or service.

PREVENTION TECHNIQUES

- Accumulate stocks of supplies and raw materials.

- Enter into futures contracts for delivery at a later date at a set price.

- Enter into long-term supply arrangements.

- Review trade publications for potential problems and/or alternate suppliers.

- Use vertical integration to reduce the price and supply risk of raw materials.

- Have the engineering staff and production managers redesign the product to reduce manufacturing costs so that the product can still be sold at the same price. If this cannot be done, redesign the existing product so that another part or different services can be supplied by another company.

- Increase the selling price of current products to determine whether the new price has a negative impact on sales. If the product must be manufactured, consumers may associate a higher price with a better-quality product and may be willing to pay more.

SPILLOVER EFFECTS. If an increased selling price causes sales to fall, the profitability of the business may remain flat or even decline. The higher selling price may diminish customer loyalty to the company's other products, resulting in an overall drop in sales and earnings. This may adversely affect the company's market share and its ability to maintain future operations. If costs of supplies and raw materials increase, profitability will decrease, unless selling prices are also increased. Cash flow will diminish because of the higher costs. If the cost of raw materials increases rapidly, production cutbacks may be necessary, resulting in less sales volume for the company's products or services. The company may lose dissatisfied customers, who may contact competitors. A company without alternative raw material or service sources possesses higher risk and uncertainty with respect to its future earnings.

Problem: Hidden Discount Costs

IDENTIFYING SYMPTOM. Failure to take a cash discount offered by suppliers who sell on short-term credit.

CAUSE. A lack of financial sophistication and/or a lack of cash.

MEASUREMENT AND ANALYSIS. An account payable is a spontaneous source of funds. Trade credit is usually extended for 30 to 60 days. Many firms attempt to extend the time for payment to take advantage of additional short-term financing. On the other hand, creditors encourage early payment by offering a cash discount. If management has not taken advantage of an available discount opportunity by paying within the appropriate discount period, it has lost an opportunity cost or the return available from an alternative use of the funds. The cost of payment within the discount period is usually higher than the cost of borrowing money.

The standard formula for computing the opportunity cost is as follows:

$$\text{Opportunity cost} = \frac{\text{discount forgone}}{\text{use of proceeds}} \times \frac{360}{\text{days use of money}}$$

Example: X Corporation purchases $500,000 of merchandise on credit terms of 2/10, net/30. The company does not pay within 10 days and thus loses the $10,000 ($500,000 × 2 percent) discount.

$$\text{Opportunity cost} = \frac{0.02 \times \$500,000}{0.98 \times \$500,000} \times \frac{360}{20}$$

$$= \frac{\$10,000 \times 180}{\$490,000} = 36.7\%$$

The cost of using the $490,000 for 20 more days is 36.7 percent. Based upon this excessive rate, management would be better off borrowing the $490,000 at the prime interest rate.

REPAIR.   Compute the opportunity cost of not taking the discount. If it is excessively high, payment should be made within the prescribed cash discount period.

PREVENTION TECHNIQUES

- Have adequate cash on hand and/or the ability to borrow on short notice to obtain the funds to pay suppliers within the discount period.
- Coordinate purchases and discount terms after determining the cash cycles of the business and the availability of money.

SPILLOVER EFFECTS.   The failure to take a discount is an opportunity cost, resulting in a larger cash payment and thus reducing cash on hand and increasing the cost of financing operations. The net effect is to lower overall liquidity and profitability.

Problem: Poor Credit Rating

IDENTIFYING SYMPTOM.   A firm's credit rating is lowered. Credit is unavailable.

CAUSES

- Market conditions
- Excessive business risk
- The quality of management
- The product mix
- Continuous operating losses
- Foreseeable future economic developments in the company's line of business
- Excessive obsolete assets
- Foreign competition
- Government action
- Failure to make a required payment on long-term debt
- Excessive interest and labor costs

- Overexpansion or diversification into other areas in which the company has no experience
- Cash flow problems
- Overall deficient financial position

MEASUREMENT AND ANALYSIS

- Evaluate the financial statement information and the overall performance of the enterprise.
- Conduct horizontal, vertical, and ratio analyses.
- Decide whether sales, income, and expenses are increasing or decreasing over time and ascertain why.
- Calculate trend percentages, which is a form of horizontal analysis.
- Study the reports in business publications.
- Learn what brokerage research reports have to say about the company.
- Compare the company's operating figures with industry norms and competitors.
- Study the company's cash flow statement.
- Calculate the liquidity and profitability ratios reflecting a company's ability to pay current liabilities, sell inventory and collect receivables, pay long-term debt, and remain profitable.
- Examine the earnings per share.

REPAIR

- Bring in outside consultants to recommend ways in which the job performance of management could be improved.
- Review the financial statements for low-quality assets and excessive operating costs.
- Evaluate production facilities for possible replacement or disposal.
- Study foreign competition, so that you can either compete better or form an operating partnership with foreign competitors to gain their expertise.
- Drop unprofitable items or sell or spin off subsidiaries that have not shown a profit over time.
- Attempt to restructure the company's debt and capital structure.
- Renegotiate union contracts for "give-backs."
- Approach creditors to modify the company's obligation to repay long-term debt.

- Reorganize to reduce diversification and enable management to gain better operating and cost control.

- If government actions are pending against the company, try to seek an out-of-court settlement to avoid negative publicity.

- Reexamine the employee benefits package to attract and keep experienced personnel.

- Consider acquiring another company that already has established markets and management capability that would enable you to expand into new geographic or product areas.

PREVENTION TECHNIQUES

- Hammer out a new corporate strategy. This involves a long-range study of the market threats and opportunities facing the company, an assessment of the company's own strengths and weaknesses, and the creation of profit goals to be achieved by each unit of the company.

- Adopt cost-cutting procedures by creating a cash budget that outlines the financial constraints the company faces and develop reasonable alternative proposals.

- Allocate resources so that management has the necessary resources to achieve its profit goals.

- Set up capital and operating budgets. The capital budget will be used to purchase new and more efficient long-lived equipment, while the operating budget will reflect expenditures for recurring costs, such as materials and salaries.

SPILLOVER EFFECTS. A firm with a lower credit rating and price per share can become a takeover candidate. The market price of the company's stock will decline. Credit will be more difficult and expensive to obtain.

Problem: Check Fraud and Improper Payments

IDENTIFYING SYMPTOMS

- Unauthorized individuals are forging checks.

- Cash disbursements are made to nonexistent suppliers or payees.

- Liabilities remain unpaid, are overpaid, or paid twice.

- The company receives an excessive amount of late payment notices, resulting both in interest charges from suppliers and penalties from governmental agencies.

- An audit reveals expenditures well above what is considered normal or has been budgeted for the accounting period.
- Independent auditors discover fraud and embezzlement.
- The company issues unnumbered checks that are not recorded in the accounting records.
- Disbursements are under the control of one individual.
- The cash balance shown in the cash account is more than the cash on hand and in the company's cash account.
- A bank reconciliation performed by the independent accountants reveals discrepancies between the book and bank balances.
- Endorsements are missing from the back of checks.
- Checks are written with spaces so that they can be later altered by payees and all subsequent holders of the instrument.
- An abnormal number of checks are payable to cash.
- Many interbank transfers cover cash shortages in the cash statements received from the bank.
- Bills are not checked for accuracy in regard to the items purchased, pricing, or total amounts.

CAUSES

- Inadequate internal control procedures
- Employee fraud

MEASUREMENT AND ANALYSIS.   Although the cash balance is not normally a major figure on the balance sheet, the volume and dollar amount that flow through the account are usually greater than any other account. In addition, cash, as the most liquid of all assets, is easily vulnerable to theft. Management must assess the risk that errors and irregularities may materially affect the company's financial statements.

REPAIR

- Review and test all internal control procedures.
- Separate the functions of authorizing payment, signing the checks, and recording them in the accounting records.
- Determine who is responsible for checking all bills and payroll records.
- Have the independent auditors perform a monthly bank reconciliation and compare the signature on the checks with the list of authorized check-signers. Examine the endorsements to see that

the check is endorsed by the payee and that there are no unusual second endorsements.

- Compare all canceled checks for several accounting periods with the accounting records as to date, number, payee, and amount.
- Investigate the reason for the large number of checks made payable to cash and any long outstanding checks.
- Seek reimbursement from the company's insurer for any actual losses sustained.
- Prosecute all perpetrators and announce this policy to the entire company.

PREVENTION TECHNIQUES

- Review, evaluate, and install new internal control procedures for cash disbursement.
- Perform a monthly bank reconciliation.
- Account for all check numbers issued during the month ending on the audit date.
- Review all interbank transfers.
- Perform a proof of cash.
- Trace all disbursements to actual purchases and to the employee payroll.
- Review all purchase requisitions to see that the company actually needed the supplies and services, that there was authorization to make the purchase, and that the goods or services were actually received.
- Keep the check writing machine under lock and key when not in use.
- Have cosigners for large checks.
- Bond all employees who are involved in signing checks and recording disbursements.
- Learn whether employees own or operate enterprises that have direct dealings with the company that might create the opportunity for collusive activities.

SPILLOVER EFFECTS. The lack of effective check authorization and disbursement procedures will cause the recording of nonexistent assets and expenses, and result in inadequate working capital due to the theft of cash. Misstatements may exist in financial position and operating results. This will lead to incorrect financial management decisions, audits, and review by various governmental agencies.

Stockholder derivative suits will be directed against the board of directors and corporate executives for mismanagement. Further, investors may sue the company for losses sustained because of the theft of cash and the preparation of erroneous financial statements. Bankruptcy is possible if the uncontrolled thefts continue.

See also RECORDKEEPING ERRORS.

Problem: Stringent Credit Requirements

IDENTIFYING SYMPTOMS

- Lost sales
- Loss of customers in higher risk categories
- Declining profitability

CAUSES

- Management conservatism
- Poor financial management and analysis
- Deficient credit analysis and evaluation
- Overall economic problems
- Industry difficulties

MEASUREMENT AND ANALYSIS. A tight credit policy is indicated by

- Declining sales
- Lower uncollectible accounts
- High accounts receivable turnover (annual credit sales divided by the average accounts receivable)
- Short collection period (360 days divided by the accounts receivable turnover rate)

Financial management is often faced with a decision of whether to give credit to marginal customers.

REPAIR. Relax the credit policy to give credit when the profitability of the additional sales that will result exceeds the additional cost associated with these sales. These costs include higher bad debts, the opportunity cost of putting funds in receivables for a longer time period, and increased clerical costs for servicing an additional customer base.

Determine the policy based on rating systems such as the Dun and Bradstreet credit rating. However, do not use a uniform standard for all customers.

PREVENTION TECHNIQUES

- Redirect credit management to consider the benefits of liberalizing credit: increased profitability, future business, and improved public relations.
- Have credit approval done by experienced and realistic credit managers.

SPILLOVER EFFECTS

- Loss of market share and competitive advantage
- Lack of growth
- Lower net income
- Worsened balance sheet position

3

Inventory Shortfalls

Failure to turn over merchandise will result in higher carrying costs and obsolescence. Tying up money in inventory balances sacrifices a return on the money. On the other hand, inadequate stocking will result in lost sales and may cause customers to switch to other suppliers. Failure to control inventory ordering and storage costs will adversely affect profitability. Inadequate internal controls will result in inventory theft. Inaccurate inventory records and miscounts will fail to reveal how much inventory actually exists. If production or supplier schedules are not adhered to, facilities may be idle and cause improper inventory balances. This may mean that the firm is frequently out of certain items and loses sales. Poor-quality goods will be reflected in product returns and discounts as well as in loss of customer satisfaction and loyalty.

Problem: Low Turnover of Merchandise

IDENTIFYING SYMPTOMS

- Slow sales.
- Unusual buildup of inventory either at the plant or at the wholesale or retail level. A buildup is indicated when inventory increases faster than sales.
- Lack of demand for products.
- Deficiencies in the product line.
- Technological obsolescence.

CAUSES. The usual reason is lack of demand. This may be due to:

- High prices
- Poor marketing efforts
- Increased competition

- Inventory purchases that exceed production and sales requirements
- Ineffective advertising
- Negative publicity

Additionally, previously written-off inventory, still on hand, may have been included in the count of ending inventory.

MEASUREMENT AND ANALYSIS.   Determine the inventory turnover by inventory category as well as by department. The inventory turnover ratio is calculated as follows:

$$\frac{\text{Cost of goods sold}}{\text{Average inventory}}$$

A seasonal business should determine the inventory turnover rate on a monthly or quarterly basis.

Example: The Fremount Corporation presents the following information for the year 19XX:

$$\text{Cost of goods sold} \quad = \$4,500,000$$

$$\text{Beginning inventory } 1/1/\text{XX} = 1,000,000$$

$$\text{Ending inventory } 12/31/\text{XX} = 800,000$$

The inventory turnover would be 5 times, calculated as follows:

Average inventory:

Beginning inventory 1/1/XX   = $1,000,000

Ending inventory 12/31/XX   =   800,000

Beginning plus ending inventory = $1,800,000

$$\text{Average inventory for year} \quad = \frac{\$1,800,000}{2} = \$900,000$$

$$\frac{\text{Cost of goods sold}}{\text{Average inventory}} = \frac{\$4,500,000}{\$900,000} = 5$$

The inventory turnover measures the number of times a company sells its average inventory during the year. A high turnover indicates a product that is selling well, whereas a low turnover indicates a lack of demand for the product. But a high inventory turnover may not necessarily be the best situation. It may instead indicate that the company is not keeping enough inventory on hand to meet sales and production demands. Having insufficient inventory on hand can mean lost production time and lost sales. Also, the turnover rate may be unrepresentatively high when the firm uses its "natural year-end," since at that time the inventory balance will be exceptionally low.

In some cases, a low turnover rate may be appropriate, as when higher inventory levels occur in anticipation of rapidly rising prices, or when a new product line has been introduced for which the advertising effects have not yet been felt.

The inventory turnover ratio varies from industry to industry. It indicates how quickly a company is selling its inventory and whether the inventory is readily marketable. By comparing the turnover ratio with other companies in the same industry, financial management can determine whether the inventory on hand is reasonable and sufficient to meet sales and production demands.

A sharp decline in the ratio over a long period mandates corrective action by management.

The number of days inventory is held should also be computed. The age of inventory should be compared to the industry norm as well as to the firm's experience.

Determine the percentage of inventory that is comprised of slow-moving, obsolete, and out-of-favor merchandise.

A decline in raw materials, coupled with an increase in work-in-process and finished goods, may indicate a future production slowdown.

REPAIR

- Compare the company's inventory turnover with other companies in the same industry and with industry averages.

- Question the sales force about why sales appear to be declining.

- Determine whether the company's advertising campaign is effective.

- Identify and discard damaged or obsolete inventory.

- Cancel purchase commitments of additional quantities of similar items.

- Check for errors in the inventory records.

- Count all items on hand prior to calculating their turnover.

- Ascertain the ideal inventory turnover number and adjust the inventory balances on hand to meet this number.

- Determine whether previously written-off inventory may still be on hand and counted in ending inventory.

- Correct the records where required.

PREVENTION TECHNIQUES

- Establish a standard of management performance by product line and compare these standards to other companies in the same industry. If the ratio is an average involving many types of goods, it may be difficult to determine which goods are selling and which are not.

- Break down all items into different categories and calculate the turnover for each category.
- Compare the company turnover amounts with other companies in the industry and with the industry average.

SPILLOVER EFFECTS.   Low inventory turnover increases the possibility of inventory obsolescence, lost sales, and theft. Excess inventory increases the costs of insurance, storage, and payroll, resulting in a drop in net earnings. Excess inventory also ties up funds that could be invested elsewhere for a return.

Problem: Deficient Inventory Balances

IDENTIFYING SYMPTOMS

- Production cutbacks
- Inability to satisfy customers

CAUSE.   Failure to use an inventory model or a computerized inventory system, resulting in orders at the wrong time and in the wrong amount.

MEASUREMENT AND ANALYSIS.   The reorder point (ROP) tells you the level of inventory at which a new order should be placed. However, to use ROP you must know the lead time from placing to receiving an order:

Reorder point = lead time × average usage per unit of time

NOTE: If you need a safety stock, then add this amount to the ROP model.

Example: Assume usage of 6400 units evenly throughout the year, and constant lead time of one week. There are 50 working weeks in the year. Reorder point is computed as follows:

$$\text{Reorder point} = 1 \text{ week} \times \frac{6{,}400}{50 \text{ weeks}} = 1 \times 128 = 128 \text{ units}$$

When the inventory level drops to 128 units, a new order should be placed.

Figure 3.1 shows this inventory system when the order quantity equals 400 units.

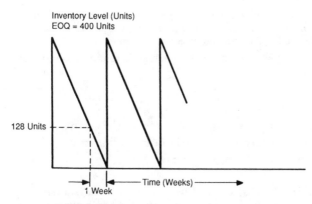

Figure 3.1 Basic inventory system.

REPAIR. Use an inventory model to determine when a reorder should be placed.

PREVENTION TECHNIQUES. Examine previous shortages, how long it usually takes to get a delivery from a supplier, seasonal demands of customers, what the usage has been, and the condition of manufacturing facilities.

SPILLOVER EFFECTS

- Losing existing and prospective customers
- Manufacturing delays
- Inactivity in productive resources
- Lower earnings

See also DELAYED RECEIPT OF NEW INVENTORY, EXCESSIVE ORDERING AND CAR-RYING COSTS, HIGH RATE OF INVENTORY STOCKOUT, and ORDERING INCORRECT QUANTITIES.

Problem: Excessive Ordering and Carrying Costs

IDENTIFYING SYMPTOMS

- Carrying costs are high because of a buildup in inventory. Carrying costs include warehousing, handling, property tax, and insurance.

- High costs per order prompt a higher order quantity each time. Order costs include the costs of preparing a purchase order and receiving goods, freight, and processing payments.
- Overstocking of inventory may result in inventory obsolescence and theft.

CAUSES

- Improper inventory management, planning, and control
- Excessive inventory balances and a lack of cost control
- Inefficient purchasing department

MEASUREMENT AND ANALYSIS.   A trade-off exists between order size and the carrying cost. The higher the order quantity, the higher the carrying cost, but the lower the ordering cost.

$$\text{Total number of orders} = \frac{S}{EOQ}$$

where S = total usage
    EOQ = economic order quantity: the optimum amount to order each time to minimize total inventory costs (ordering and carrying)

$$\text{Total order cost} = \frac{S}{EOQ} \times O$$

where O = cost per order

$$\text{Total carrying cost} = \frac{EOQ}{2} \times C$$

where C = carrying cost per unit

$$\frac{EOQ}{2} = \text{average inventory quantity for the period}$$

$$\text{Total inventory cost} = \frac{(S \times O)}{EOQ} + \frac{(EOQ \times C)}{2}$$

Compare the trend in carrying costs and ordering costs over time. Determine the ratio of carrying cost to inventory, carrying cost to sales, ordering cost to inventory, and ordering cost to sales. Higher ratios may signal problems.

Inventory levels are also influenced by short-term interest rates. As interest rates increase, it costs more to finance and hold inventory.

REPAIR

- Hold less physical inventory.
- Place fewer orders.

- Determine the optimal inventory level necessary to minimize related costs by using inventory models.

- Reduce production until the proper inventory levels are reached.

- Use the just-in-time (JIT) system of managing inventory, in which the company buys and produces in very small quantities *just in time* for use, so as to reduce inventory costs.

- Purchase large volumes to get greater purchase discounts.

- Streamline clerical operations.

- Hold lower inventory balances and rent cheaper storage space.

- Move to a lower-taxed locality.

- Reduce insurance costs by altering the deductible, changing policy limits, or switching to a new insurance carrier.

- Place stringent internal controls over inventory to guard against theft.

PREVENTION TECHNIQUES

- Establish policies to achieve the optimal inventory balance to reduce costs.

- Use the reorder point model (ROP) to know when to order.

- Compute average sales volume per square foot of shelf space, and replace products whose sales are grossly below the average.

- Redesign packaging to save costs.

SPILLOVER EFFECTS.   High costs associated with inventory will result in lower profit margins. Deficient inventory planning will cause inventory losses due to oversupply, obsolescence, perishability, and so on.

See also DEFICIENT INVENTORY BALANCES, HIGH RATE OF INVENTORY STOCKOUT, and ORDERING INCORRECT QUANTITIES.

Problem: Ordering Incorrect Quantities

IDENTIFYING SYMPTOMS

- Overstocking

- Obsolescence

- Shortages

- Back orders

- Production slowdowns

- Inventory theft

CAUSES

- The wrong amount of inventory is ordered because of poor inventory management and control.
- Inventory models are not in use.

MEASUREMENT AND ANALYSIS.   One technique that can be used to order the right amount is the EOQ model. It determines the order size that minimizes the sum of carrying and ordering costs. The EOQ model is suitable for a pure inventory system; that is, for single-item, single-stage inventory decisions for which joint costs and constraints can be ignored. (EOQ does not consider quantity discounts, which may be unrealistic. Typically, the more you order, the lower the unit price you pay.)

EOQ assumes that demand is known with certainty and will remain constant throughout the year. Order cost and unit carrying costs are also assumed to be constant. Since demand and lead time (time interval between placing an order and receiving delivery) are assumed to be determinable, no shortage costs exist.

EOQ is computed as follows:

$$EOQ = \sqrt{\frac{2 \, (\text{annual demand}) \, (\text{ordering cost})}{\text{carrying cost per unit}}}$$

$$\text{Total inventory costs} = \text{carrying cost per unit} \times \frac{EOQ}{2} + \text{order cost}$$

$$\times \frac{\text{annual demand}}{EOQ}$$

$$\text{Total number of orders per year} = \frac{\text{annual demand}}{EOQ}$$

Example: Oakman, Inc. buys sets of steel at $40 per set from an outside vendor. Oakman will need 6400 sets evenly throughout the year. Management desires a 16 percent return on its inventory investment (cost of capital). In addition, rent, insurance, taxes, etc. for each set in inventory comes to $1.60. The order cost is $100.

The carrying cost per set = $1.60 + 16% (40) = $8.00.

Thus,

$$EOQ = \sqrt{\frac{2(6,400)(100)}{\$8.00}}$$

$$= \sqrt{160,000} = 400 \text{ sets}$$

Total inventory costs = $8.00 (400/2) + $100 (6400/400)

$$= \$1,600 + \$1,600 = \$3,200$$

Total number of annual orders = 6,400/400

$$= 16 \text{ orders}$$

REPAIR.   Use the EOQ model to determine order size and frequency of orders. Increase order size to take advantage of quantity discounts or lower prices.

PREVENTION TECHNIQUES

- Improve forecasting and recordkeeping.
- Use EOQ formulas.
- Hire an experienced inventory manager.

SPILLOVER EFFECTS.   Incorrect order size leads either to an inventory buildup or to inadequate inventory levels. An inventory buildup results in excess carrying costs, drain on cash flow, obsolescence and spoilage, increased theft, and lower profitability. An inadequate inventory balance will result in lost sales and customer dissatisfaction.

See also DEFICIENT INVENTORY BALANCES, EXCESSIVE ORDERING AND CARRYING COSTS, and HIGH RATE OF INVENTORY STOCKOUT.

Problem: High Rate of Inventory Stockout

IDENTIFYING SYMPTOM.   No merchandise to fill customer orders.

CAUSE.   Poor inventory planning and control due to inaccurate estimates of sales or materials requirements.

MEASUREMENT AND ANALYSIS.   When lead time and demand are uncertain, you must carry extra units of inventory, called *safety stock,* as protection against possible stockouts. Safety stock is the minimum inventory amount needed to serve as a safety buffer against unusual product demand or unanticipated delivery problems.

The optimal safety stock is the one in which increased carrying cost equals the opportunity cost applicable to a possible stockout. The increased carrying cost equals the carrying cost per unit times the safety stock.

Stockout cost = Number of orders (S/EOQ) × stockout units

× unit stockout cost × probability of a stockout

Example: You use 250,000 units per year. Each order is for 25,000 units. Stockout is 4000 units. The tolerable stockout probability is 25 percent. The per-unit stockout cost is $4. The carrying cost per unit is $8.

$$\text{Stockout cost} = \frac{250,000}{25,000} \times 4000 \times \$4 \times 0.25 = \$40,000$$

$$\text{Amount of safety stock needed} = \frac{\text{Stockout cost}}{\text{Carrying cost per unit}}$$

$$= \frac{\$40,000}{\$8} = 5000 \text{ units}$$

$$\text{EOP} = SL + F\sqrt{S(\text{EOQ})(L)}$$

where L = Lead time
F = Stockout acceptance factor

A stockout cost is estimated at $12 per set. The carrying cost is $8 per set. The reorder point is 128 sets without considering safety stock. Computation of safety stock is shown in the table below.

The table shows that total costs are minimized at $1200 when a safety stock of 150 sets is maintained. Thus, ROP = 128 sets + 150 sets, or 278 sets.

Safety stock levels in units	Stockout and probability	Average stockout in units	Average stockout costs	No. of orders	Total annual stockout costs	Carrying costs	Total
0	50 with .2 100 with .1 150 with .1	35*	$420†	16	$6720‡	0	$6720
50	50 with .1 100 with .1	15	180	16	2880	400§	3280
100	50 with .1	5	60	16	960	800	1760
150	0	0	0	16	0	1200	1200

*50(.2) + 100(.1) + 150(.1) = 10 + 10 + 15 = 35 units
†35 units × $12.00 = $420
‡$420 × 16 times = $6,720
§50 units × $8.00 = $400

REPAIR

- Order additional inventory of selected items to guard against stockouts.

- Introduce computerized systems, such as material requirements planning (MRP), which involves having enough materials on hand to meet expected future demand.

PREVENTION TECHNIQUES.   Use the above formulas to determine the stockout cost, safety stock, and reorder point.

SPILLOVER EFFECTS

- Lost sales
- Reduced profits
- Disgruntled customers
- Idle machines
- Disrupted production scheduling

See also DEFICIENT INVENTORY BALANCES, and EXCESSIVE ORDERING AND CARRYING COSTS.

Problem: Theft

IDENTIFYING SYMPTOM.   Inventory on hand is less than what is indicated in the accounting records.

CAUSES

- Lack of physical safeguards
- Improper internal control
- Inaccurate accounting records
- Failure to record inventory purchases
- Ineffective or inaccurate method of counting inventory

MEASUREMENT AND ANALYSIS.   Management and outside auditors have performed a physical count of the inventory and have determined which inventory is actually owned by the company and which is held in a custodial capacity for other companies. The amount per books does not reconcile with the amount actually on hand. Inventory shortages may require immediate purchase of the missing items to meet urgent customer demands, thereby exposing the purchasing company to higher prices plus premium transportation costs for rush delivery of the goods. Thus, the thefts create additional unnecessary expense.

REPAIR

- Review all internal control procedures.
- Conduct training programs for each inventory procedure.
- Have each inventory item assigned to a different area with a specific person in charge.
- Lock up all merchandise.
- Install a lock system permitting limited access to low-cost inventory by one authorized individual and a two-key system requiring two or more authorized employees for higher-value inventory.
- File insurance claims to recover the cost of stolen inventory.
- Carefully mark, "Do Not Inventory," and segregate, if possible, all material that was sold before the end of the accounting period to avoid inclusion in the ending inventory count.

PREVENTION TECHNIQUES

- Install proper internal control procedures.
- Inspect all inventory purchased and received by the company to check whether it actually received the amount indicated on the vendor's bill.
- Establish a system whereby different employees accept purchased goods; transfer the goods to the warehouse, other storage area, or production line; keep inventory records; and ship merchandise to customers.
- Make unannounced spot counts of the inventory on hand.
- Make the employee in charge explain any discrepancies.
- Change locks or security codes in storage areas periodically.
- Make theft-awareness everyone's responsibility, so that any employee can furnish information without fear of reprisal.
- Encourage employees to report possible weaknesses in the inventory security system.
- Bond all employees associated with the inventory's physical storage and recordkeeping.
- Maintain a well-prepared perpetual computerized inventory system to enable the company to better control inventory.
- Determine whether all inventory purchases have been validly authorized.

SPILLOVER EFFECTS. Theft of inventory can cause a serious decline in profits and possible insolvency and bankruptcy. The company will lose customers if management tells potential purchasers that they have certain inventory on hand when in fact it is missing. Management could be sued by the stockholders for incompetence and negligence regarding inventory, a major asset on the balance sheet. The disclosure of employee fraud will increase audit fees.

Problem: Miscounted Inventory

IDENTIFYING SYMPTOMS

- Unusually large balances in obsolete goods.
- Small balances in current inventory parts.
- No balances for parts that are usually in stock at all times.
- Inventory held in a custodial capacity for other owners and counted as part of the ending inventory.

CAUSES

- Inexperienced help
- Lack of training in counting of inventory
- Improper inventory identification procedures
- A shortage of qualified personnel
- Improper entries
- Math errors

MEASUREMENT AND ANALYSIS

- Assign an experienced and reliable inventory counter to review all inventory tickets and forms for accuracy in describing and counting the items on hand.
- Have another experienced employee double-check all inventory tickets for correct quantities.
- Correct any tickets found to contain errors.

REPAIR

- Establish a definite procedure for classifying and counting inventory.
- Employ only experienced people familiar with the raw materials used in production to count the inventory.

- Go back and physically recount a percentage of all major balances of inventory and a small percentage of the lower value items.

- Question management and employees about goods held by others on consignment or in a warehouse at another location.

- Use a "commonsense test" if the count looks suspicious.

- Make out a zero-quantity tag for items with an assigned location but no parts.

- Consolidate all similar items to expedite accurate control and count.

PREVENTION TECHNIQUES

- Prepare an inventory policy. This policy should contain lessons on the purpose of the inventory program, responsibilities in the chain of command, a brief discussion of the reasons why an accurate inventory count is important, and examples of errors, their causes, and their negative impact on the company's financial status.

- Define the role of the inventory coordinator. This individual should have experience in creating inventory policy and writing inventory procedures, including the counting of ending inventory.

- Review the status of ending inventory balances; check the accuracy of the number of parts received; appraise employee performance in the periodic counting of inventory; and monitor inventory balances for discrepancies.

- Use a uniform inventory ticket for listing the actual amount on hand. Use one tag for each inventory item. Number all tags and account for missing ones at the end of the count. Have employees initial the ticket.

- If tag corrections make tags illegible, mark them "VOID," write a new tag, and give voided and unused tags to the inventory coordinator. Number all inventory sheets and account for all missing sheets at the end of the count. Double-count all high-value items.

- Be sure employees understand inventory instructions. Review the results of the final inventory count for unusual deviations from what is considered a normal ending balance for a specific part or selection of parts.

- Supervise inventory counts carefully. No requisitions should be permitted without special permission of the inventory coordinator. Make sure that inventory that must be moved during the counting period is not counted twice. No movement of material within an area should be done without authorization by the area supervisor.

- Post instructions for calibration and weigh counting directly on the scales.

SPILLOVER EFFECTS.   If ending inventory is incorrect, the company's understanding of its profits, balance sheet, tax liabilities, current ratio, and working capital will also be incorrect.

Problem: Inaccurate Inventory Records

IDENTIFYING SYMPTOMS

- Inability to meet delivery promises
- Uneven production due to lack of inventory
- Excessive machine downtime because of material shortages
- Incomplete records
- Duplication of effort
- Unproductive recordkeeping time
- Theft of inventory
- An increase in audit fees
- Confusion caused by inventory held for another company and erroneously included with the company's own ending inventory
- Overlapping accounting functions

CAUSES

- Incompetent or inexperienced accounting staff
- Shortage of qualified employees
- Lack of internal controls and audits
- Deficient organizational structure
- Failure to keep up-to-date records
- Failure to identify inventory consigned to the company for resale that belongs to other companies

MEASUREMENT AND ANALYSIS.   Inaccurate inventory records affect management decisions and net income. Management must analyze the composition of the inventory in terms of inventory items on hand, the service level—that is, the percent of the time that inventory will be on the shelf to meet a customer's requirements—and the incidence and dollar amount of inventory theft. Recordkeeping errors misstate inventory.

REPAIR

- Institute internal controls to safeguard assets and assure the integrity of the accounting system.

- Improve unsatisfactory procedures.

- Check for inconsistencies in the inventory procedures.

- Undertake internal and external audits to confirm the accuracy of the inventory records. Any accounting errors discovered should be corrected immediately.

- Ask an independent CPA firm to evaluate the accounting system and make written recommendations for improvement.

- Install computerized inventory software packages and a bar code system to improve the accuracy and timeliness of the records.

PREVENTION TECHNIQUES

- Implement in-house training programs to assure that the accounting staff understands how to operate the computer program and the bar-code system.

- Ensure employee honesty and competency.

- Institute a clear separation of duties to ensure proper internal control.

- Make sure all accounting procedures are properly authorized.

- Make sure that all transactions are properly documented and reviewed. This should include specific authorizations for certain individual transactions.

- Establish adequate control over physical assets and records.

- Create safeguards to prevent misappropriation of inventory.

- Have independent checks by both internal and external auditors to ensure that inventory balances on hand agree with accounting records.

- Assign designated items of inventory to specific areas for easy identification. The person responsible for a particular inventory storage area must be able to explain any discrepancies.

SPILLOVER EFFECTS.   If the inventory accounting system is inadequate or inefficient, it will not generate reliable information. The result will be faulty financial decisions based on inaccurate data. The cost of goods sold and ending inventory, major components of both the balance sheet and income statement, will be wrong. As a result, misstatements may exist in the financial position and operating results of the company. This will lead to poor decisions, audits and review by various governmental agencies, and lawsuits by stockholders, investors, and creditors. These actions will negatively affect the market price of the company's outstanding shares and subsequent public offerings.

See also RECORDKEEPING ERRORS.

Problem: High Rate of Product Obsolescence

IDENTIFYING SYMPTOMS

- Low inventory turnover
- Slow sales despite large markdowns
- New competing models with advanced features

CAUSES

- Perishable, specialized, faddish, or high-tech products
- Excess purchasing without specific production goals
- Errors in production requirements
- Sudden lack of demand for the product
- Purchase of a large amount of goods because of advantageous purchasing terms

MEASUREMENT AND ANALYSIS.   Evaluate the age and write-downs of older and less desirable merchandise.

REPAIR

- Create an advisory group familiar with the manufacturing requirements of the business to advise top management on policy-making decisions.
- Set a specific inventory level for production and sales purposes.
- Determine a proper level of inventory based on the company's turnover and production objectives.
- Determine the existence of damaged, slow moving, overstocked, out-of-style, and obsolete inventories, looking for commitments of additional quantities of similar items. If advisable, cancel these commitments.
- Sell off obsolete inventory at the market price. If the inventory has no value, donate it to a local charity to generate goodwill and

favorable publicity. Its disposal will allow the company to reduce the costs of storage, warehousing, insurance coverage, and payroll incurred in recordkeeping and safeguarding the obsolete inventory.

- Determine whether the recent shipments of obsolete inventory can be returned to vendors for partial or complete credit.

PREVENTION TECHNIQUES

- Determine a proper inventory level. An excellent method to use is the targeted inventory method, under which the total inventory issues in dollars for the prior year are divided by the inventory turnover desired by management. The result is the inventory target amount, which is then compared to the actual inventory on hand. If the actual amount exceeds the targeted inventory amount, the excess is deemed excess inventory, subject to possible obsolescence.

Example:

Total inventory purchases last year = $5,000,000

Turnover desired by management = 25

Actual inventory at year-end = $ 222,000

The excess inventory on hand at year-end subject to possible obsolescence would be $22,000, calculated as follows:

Inventory target ($5,000,000 ÷ 25) = $200,000

Actual inventory at year-end = 222,000

Excess inventory subject to possible obsolescence = $ 22,000

- Establish an inventory reduction group that will review all areas and activities affecting the factory and warehouse inventory levels. Have the group review and analyze inventory management problems and suggest immediate and obvious steps to reduce inventories.
- Classify inventory target categories into desirable, permissible, and nondesirable levels.
- Carefully reduce inventory levels to a predetermined minimum without affecting production or the service level to customers.
- Allow management to determine which level is preferable for maintaining a proper production schedule and service level to customers.
- Study industry trends in product changes, supplies of raw materials, and manufacturing processes.

- Attempt to negotiate a liberal return policy on inventory purchases with suppliers.

SPILLOVER EFFECTS. The writedown of obsolete inventory will increase the cost of goods sold and will lower earnings.

Problem: Missed Manufacturing Schedules

IDENTIFYING SYMPTOMS

- Production quotas and schedules are not met.
- Sales orders are not filled because completed inventory is not available for immediate shipment.
- Sales are declining.
- The company is getting a reputation for unreliability.
- Raw materials are delayed, resulting in significant downtime, with both workers and machines idle.
- Production facilities are obsolete.
- Workers are inexperienced and unproductive.

CAUSES

- Inexperienced personnel
- Product technological innovations requiring retraining
- Introduction of new production machinery and methods
- Failure to forecast inventory requirements and keep purchases at a correct level
- Stockouts of required parts
- Excessive employee absences and turnover
- High rate of customer turnover and order cancellations
- Theft of vital materials

MEASUREMENT AND ANALYSIS. Efficient companies review their production proficiency every three months because of technological changes in the marketplace, the introduction of new production equipment, the availability of raw materials, and changes in the availability of experienced personnel. The review should consist of an appraisal of the organizational structure, production objectives, inventory control methods, effectiveness of the various production departments, and the accuracy of the accounting records.

REPAIR

- Determine the weaknesses in each sector of the company associated with the production process.
- Evaluate the performance of production managers, supervisors, and workers.
- Establish safety stock levels.
- Make sure that rejected material purchases are quickly returned to vendors or reprocessed.
- Monitor employee absenteeism and turnover.
- Evaluate all personnel performance associated with inventory management.

PREVENTION TECHNIQUES

- Establish production goals by division or product lines to meet customer needs.
- Develop methods for efficient purchase procedures.
- Make sure that engineering changes in production facilities are quickly implemented.
- Define production responsibility and lines of authority.
- Standardize inventory parts and production procedures where possible.
- Adjust salaries and increase employee benefits where necessary.
- Seek suggestions for improvements in manufacturing procedures from production personnel and shop supervisors.
- Make sure that materials in inventory are available and are properly identified.
- Institute quick inspection and rejection procedures for all materials-receiving departments.
- Ensure that vendors are paid on time, so that they will respond quickly to future company purchase requests.
- Establish procedures for protecting inventory from theft.

SPILLOVER EFFECTS

- Inventory stockouts
- Inability to meet customer sales

- Increased insurance, storage, and administrative costs
- Decline in net earnings

See also HIGH RATE OF PRODUCT OBSOLESCENCE, INACCURATE INVENTORY RECORDS, and LOW TURNOVER OF MERCHANDISE.

Problem: Poor-Quality Goods

IDENTIFYING SYMPTOMS

- Excessive returns of merchandise
- Discounts given to customers to keep goods
- Declining sales and market share
- A reputation for shoddy quality and workmanship

CAUSES

- Obsolete production facilities
- New, inexperienced, or unproductive workers
- Poor-quality materials
- Scheduling problems
- Cutting corners on materials and workmanship
- Failure to inspect materials prior to their introduction into the manufacturing process
- Poor quality control and lack of inspection procedures
- Substitution of improper parts
- Ignorance or violation of federal, state, and local regulations governing the application of product safety standards
- Failure to investigate consumer complaints
- Improper packaging of goods, causing damage to products while in transit to customers
- Mislabeling of goods, causing customers to expect a better-quality product than the item actually purchased
- Arrogance or complacency toward the purchasing public

MEASUREMENT AND ANALYSIS

- Determine the trend in sales returns and allowances to sales. An increasing trend indicates quality problems and unhappy customers.

- Compare returns to industry norms and those of competing companies.
- Create a group familiar with the manufacturing operations of the business to advise top management on quality control.
- Set specific standards of quality control.
- Evaluate the product inspection process.
- Review packaging techniques.

REPAIR

- Determine the weaknesses in each sector of the company associated with the production process.
- Evaluate the performance of production managers, supervisors, and workers.
- Formulate and announce a stated policy of quality control.
- Inspect goods at key points during processing.
- Establish a program to replenish parts if they fall below a predetermined level.
- Update production facilities that are obsolete.
- Retrain and motivate workers regarding the need for quality workmanship.
- Change suppliers if a vendor's materials are inferior or contain inordinate defects.
- Set reasonable production timetables.
- Eliminate the cutting of corners on materials and workmanship.
- Inspect raw materials before their introduction into the manufacturing process.
- Seek the advice of legal counsel and product engineers about safety standards that the product must meet.
- Respond to consumer complaints.
- Redesign the packaging of goods and select a new delivery company, if necessary.
- Change misleading labels on goods.
- Discontinue products associated with low quality or unreliability.
- Create and promote new products with a reputation for high quality and reliability at an affordable price.

PREVENTION TECHNIQUES

- Review production proficiency and quality control every three months. The review should consist of an appraisal of the organizational structure, production objectives, and inventory control methods.

- Evaluate all personnel performance associated with production.
- Establish a committee to review consumer complaints.
- Redesign the packaging of goods.
- Monitor the performance of the delivery company for complaints regarding customers' receipt of damaged goods.
- Hire product engineers to review safety standards in the product-manufacturing process.
- Standardize the labels on goods.
- Establish an advertising campaign to improve the image of the product in the minds of the consuming public.
- Make all employees aware that consumer approval of the company's products is vital to the company's economic survival.

SPILLOVER EFFECTS.   Poor-quality goods will cause sales and net earnings to decline and seriously damage the company's image. Competitors will take away market share. Violating product safety standards can lead to government intervention and high legal costs.

See also HIGH RATE OF PRODUCT OBSOLESCENCE, INACCURATE INVENTORY RECORDS, and LOW TURNOVER OF MERCHANDISE.

Problem: Lack of Storage Space

IDENTIFYING SYMPTOMS

- Decrease in production efficiency
- Missed production deadlines
- Missing parts
- Theft and damage to inventory
- Storage space far from production facilities, resulting in delays and excessive transportation and handling costs

CAUSES

- Incorrect sales forecasts
- Improper production planning
- Obsolete facilities
- Lack of money to buy or build additional storage facilities
- Rental storage space unavailable

- High rental cost of storage space
- Failure to define managerial responsibility for the control and storage of inventory

MEASUREMENT AND ANALYSIS

- Prepare a forecast of storage requirements based on production schedules.
- Analyze storage bottlenecks, how materials are transported from storage areas to the production line, the distance they have to travel, and their weight and size.
- Study how the inventory is safeguarded while in storage.
- Ascertain the frequency of emergency customer orders, so that extra inventory can be kept on hand.
- Determine the storage space needed to accommodate production schedules.

REPAIR

- Analyze the warehouse facilities to document all physical characteristics.
- Determine the quantity and effective capacity of storage containers and bins currently in use.
- Draft a detailed layout of the storage facilities, noting all movable and immovable objects.
- Observe how storeroom employees stock and pull goods.
- Investigate access and security to storage area.
- Identify problems in the handling of goods.
- Determine how much of the inventory is obsolete or damaged and dispose of it at once to create additional storage space.
- Define managerial responsibility for the control and storage of inventory.

PREVENTION TECHNIQUES

- Purchase adjustable shelves that slide on floor rollers for smaller parts to save space.
- Install carousel-type racks to lessen square-footage space requirements.
- Use all open space at the top of the room by installing taller racks.

- Standardize package size.
- Rent storage space to best serve consumer markets.
- Stock products at appropriate locations.
- Determine the proper level for all inventory parts and set up a computer system that gives immediate warning of both understocking and overstocking.
- Set up procedures that safeguard the inventory and prevent damage.

SPILLOVER EFFECTS. Insufficient storage space will create shortage of materials, production downtime, inventory stockouts, theft, and an inability to meet emergency customer orders. These problems will cause declining sales and net earnings.

See also INACCURATE INVENTORY RECORDS.

Problem: Delayed Receipt of New Inventory

IDENTIFYING SYMPTOMS

- Lack of critical information regarding production requirements and goals.
- Continuous stockouts, shortages of materials, and missed production goals.
- Above-industry costs for placing inventory orders.
- Lack of management knowledge of the type and quantity of materials held at the company's various storage sites, causing confusion and materials shortages at key areas.

CAUSES

- Inadequate inventory distribution system
- Untrained or inexperienced personnel
- Lack of interface between manufacturing and purchase order systems
- The generation of irrelevant and confusing information regarding purchase requirements
- Problems with suppliers
- Lost or unclear orders

MEASUREMENT AND ANALYSIS

- Analyze the efficiency of the existing inventory purchase system.
- Establish a chart of managerial responsibility for the acquisition and inspection of goods.
- Determine which suppliers are honest and reliable.
- Establish when specific items of inventory must be reordered.

REPAIR

- Design and implement a new inventory acquisition system.
- Reduce the number of employees involved in the reordering process to prevent overlapping of functions.
- Retrain current employees in correct purchase methodology.
- Select the best supplier and eliminate those vendors who ship damaged inventory or fail to deliver the requested goods on time.
- Select suppliers closer to the company's manufacturing facilities to promote quick delivery of ordered goods.
- Set up a system of quotes that obtains the goods quickly at the best prices.
- Analyze all inventory parts according to predetermined classes of period usage. Use this data to set up a system of automatic reordering.
- Study shipment procedures to determine which trucking companies are reliable and deliver the ordered goods on time.
- Renegotiate contracts with suppliers to penalize them for late deliveries.

PREVENTION TECHNIQUES

- Install a purchasing structure utilizing the economic ordering quantity (EOQ) system.
- Maintain a computerized database for all inventory parts. Use it to standardize ordering requirements, amounts usually ordered, and the average amount of usage for all materials during a given production period.
- Where feasible, implement a computerized purchasing system that automatically requests the purchase of a part when supplies fall below a specific amount. Consolidate all similar goods at one location to promote an efficient reordering system.
- Define employee responsibilities for purchases. An updated pur-

chasing system should reduce inventory-related paperwork, facilitate the implementation of coordinated purchasing, reduce the time it takes to receive ordered goods, and improve communication among all company personnel involved in production.

- Give vendors a list of trucking companies that are deemed reliable and demand that these companies be used when shipping goods to the purchaser.

SPILLOVER EFFECTS.   Delayed receipt of new inventory will cause scheduling problems in manufacturing, as well as inventory stockouts, inability to meet customer sales requests, production downtime, and declining sales. Net earnings will decline.

See also INACCURATE INVENTORY RECORDS, LOW TURNOVER OF MERCHANDISE, and POOR-QUALITY GOODS.

4

Profit and
Contribution
Margin Analysis
Is Off

A company must break even to avoid losses on products or services. Breaking even means that total revenue equals total cost, resulting in zero profit. Losses may arise when costs are excessive relative to production volume. Cost controls may be needed. There may also exist a poor sales mix in the product or service line. Unprofitable business segments drain earnings and corporate resources. A loss on a contract can have a devastating effect on the bottom line. Product modification or refinement should not have adverse consequences on quantity, quality, or profitability.

Problem: Unrealistic Break-Even Point

IDENTIFYING SYMPTOM. The calculated break-even number is much higher or lower than expected.

CAUSE. A faulty break-even point is due to a higher or lower than realistic fixed cost or contribution margin.

MEASUREMENT AND ANALYSIS. The guidelines for breaking even dictate that an increase in selling price lowers break-even sales; an increase in variable cost increases break-even sales; and an increase in fixed cost increases break-even sales. One way to determine whether the break-even point is unrealistic is to calculate the margin of safety (the difference between the actual sales and the break-even sales). The margin of safety is the amount by which sales revenue may drop before losses begin, and is expressed as a percentage of expected sales as follows:

$$\text{Margin of safety} = \frac{\text{expected sales} - \text{break-even sales}}{\text{expected sales}}$$

The margin of safety is used to measure operating risk. The larger the ratio, the safer the situation, since there is less risk of reaching the break-even point.

Break-even analysis. The givens of break-even analysis are as follows.

- The selling price is constant, which in turn requires the following assumptions:

  The demand elasticity is very high for selling price to remain the same when sales volume increases. (The demand elasticity refers to the percentage change in product demand relative to the percentage change in price.)

  The selling price is stable over the income period.

- There is only one product or a constant sales mix.

- Manufacturing efficiency is constant.

- Inventories do not materially change from period to period.

- The variable cost per unit is constant. (A variable cost is one that varies with volume, such as materials.)

- The total fixed cost is constant. (A fixed cost is one that remains constant regardless of activity, such as rent and insurance.)

- The fixed cost and variable cost are properly segregated.

Example: Assume Porter Toy Stores Incorporated projects sales of $35,000 with a break-even sales level of $25,000. The projected margin of safety is

$$\frac{\$35,000 - \$25,000}{\$35,000} = 28.57\%$$

Cash break-even point. If a company has a minimum of available cash or if the opportunity cost of holding excess cash is high, the enterprise may want to determine the sales volume needed to cover all cash expenses during a period. Not all fixed costs require cash payment. (Depreciation expense is an example.) *What to do:* In coming up with the cash break-even point, reduce fixed cost by the noncash charges. Hence, the cash break-even point will be less than the usual break-even point.

Example: The selling price is $40, the variable cost per unit is $10, and the fixed cost is $64,000 (including depreciation of $4000).

Cash break-even units are calculated as follows:

$$\frac{\text{Fixed costs} - \text{depreciation}}{\text{Contribution margin per unit}} = \frac{\$64,000 - \$4000}{\$40 - \$10} = \frac{\$60,000}{\$30} = 2000 \text{ units}$$

REPAIR.   Recalculate the break-even numbers obtained in the mea-surement and analysis section. If the calculated values do not match the current values, correct the product values to give a proper break-even.

PREVENTION TECHNIQUES.   Reaffirm the company's fixed cost and contribution margin before calculating the break-even point.

SPILLOVER EFFECTS.   If the price of the product is too low, profits may decline. If it is too high, sales may fall. Declining profits and falling sales may adversely affect the company's stock price, bond offerings, market share, cost of financing, and ability to maintain future operations. Costs will have to be reduced, requiring the elimi-nation of certain nonessential (and perhaps essential) operations and personnel. An unprofitable company will be forced to lay off workers. The possibility of insolvency and bankruptcy may also increase.

See also PRODUCT OR SERVICE DOES NOT BREAK EVEN, POOR-QUALITY EARNINGS, and REVENUE BASE EROSION.

Problem: Product or Service Does Not Break Even

IDENTIFYING SYMPTOMS

- The product or service is not generating a profit.
- Earnings are decreasing with increased sales. At the calculated break-even point, the company should show zero profit/zero loss for the product.
- The company shows a financial loss at any point in a product's life.

CAUSES

- Excessive production costs
- A selling price that does not yield enough profits
- Production quantity that is too high or too low
- Poor general economic conditions, causing lower customer demand for the product or service
- Unprofitable product mix. A product line that has a high positive correlation puts the company at great risk, since the demand for all the products move in one direction. Further, products with elastic demand can experience significant changes in quantity with only modest changes in price.

- A high debt structure, which results in high fixed interest charges.

- A product that is highly price elastic, so an increase in selling price results in a sharp decline in profits.

- Reduced sales of the product, which places the units sold below the expected break-even level.

- A product with a higher variable cost than was initially calculated.

MEASUREMENT AND ANALYSIS. Cost-volume-profit analysis relates to the way in which profit and costs change with a change in production volume. It examines the impact on earnings of changes in such factors as variable cost, fixed cost, selling price, volume, and product mix. It thus aids in the planning process. Break-even analysis is useful when starting a new project, expanding a project, or subtracting from the project.

A company's business objective is not just to break even, but to earn a profit. An enterprise can extend break-even analysis to concentrate on a desired earnings figure. To compute the break-even point, we consider fixed cost (FC) and variable cost (VC) along with the following important concepts:

1. *Contribution Margin (CM).* The contribution margin is the excess of sales (S) over the variable costs (VC) of the product or service. It is the amount of money available to cover fixed costs (FC) and to generate profit. Symbolically, CM = S − VC.

2. *Unit CM.* The unit CM is the excess of the unit selling price (p) over the unit variable cost (v). Symbolically, unit CM = p − v.

3. *CM Ratio.* The CM ratio is the contribution margin as a percentage of sales:

$$\text{CM ratio} = \frac{\text{CM}}{\text{S}} = \frac{\text{S} - \text{VC}}{\text{S}} = 1 \frac{\text{VC}}{\text{S}}$$

The CM ratio can also be computed using per-unit data:

$$\text{CM ratio} = \frac{\text{Unit CM}}{\text{p}} = \frac{\text{p} - \text{v}}{\text{p}} = 1 \frac{\text{v}}{\text{p}}$$

Note that the CM ratio is 1 minus the variable cost ratio. For example, if variable costs account for 70 percent of the price, the CM ratio is 30 percent.

Example 1: To illustrate the various concepts of CM and calculate the break-even point, consider the following data for Porter Toy Stores, Incorporated:

	Total	Per unit	Percentage
Sales (1500 units)	$37,500	$25	100%
Less: Variable costs	15,000	10	40
Contribution margin	$22,500	$15	60%
Less: Fixed costs	15,000		
Net income	$7,500		

From the data listed above, CM, unit CM, and the CM ratio are computed as:

$$CM = S - VC = \$37,500 - \$15,000 = \$22,500$$

Unit $CM = p - v = \$25 - \$10 = \$15$

$$\text{CM ratio} = \frac{CM}{S} = \frac{\$22,500}{\$37,500} = 60\% \text{ or } \frac{\text{Unit CM}}{p} = \frac{\$15}{\$25} = 0.6 = 60\%$$

The break-even point represents the level of sales revenue that equals the total of the variable and fixed costs for a given volume of output at a particular capacity use rate. For example, management might want to ask the break-even occupancy rate (or vacancy rate) for a hotel or the break-even load rate for an airliner.

Generally, other things being equal, the higher the break-even point, the lower the profit and the greater the operating risk. The break-even point also provides financial managers with insights into profit planning. It can be computed using the following formulas:

$$\text{Break-even point in units} = \frac{\text{Fixed costs}}{\text{Unit CM}}$$

$$\text{Break-even point in dollars} = \frac{\text{Fixed costs}}{\text{CM ratio}}$$

Example 2: Using the same data given in Example 1, where unit CM = $25 − $10 = $15 and CM ratio = 60%, we get:

Break-even point in units = $15,000/$15 = 1000 units

Break-even point in dollars = $15,000/0.6 = $25,000

Or, alternatively,

$$1000 \text{ units} \times \$25 = \$25,000$$

Example 3: A manager is thinking of making a product that is currently purchased from outside suppliers for $0.12 per unit. The fixed cost is $10,000, and the variable cost per unit is $0.08. The number of units that have to be sold so that the annual cost of the machine equals the outside purchase cost is:

$$\frac{\text{Fixed costs}}{\text{CM per Unit}} = \frac{\$10,000}{\$0.12 - \$.08} = \frac{\$10,000}{\$.04} = 250,000 \text{ units}$$

Example 4:   Assume the following:

Selling price   = $40

Variable cost   = $24

Fixed cost   = $150,000

After-tax profit = $240,000

Tax rate   = 40%

A company wants to determine how many units it must sell to make after-tax profits.

$$\text{Desired units} = \frac{\text{Fixed costs + before-tax profit}}{\text{Contribution margin (CM) per unit}}$$

$$\frac{\$150,000 + \$400,000^*}{\$40 - \$24} = \frac{\$550,000}{\$16} = 34,375 \text{ units}$$

Sales mix.   Break-even analysis requires additional computations when more than one product is produced and sold. Different selling prices and different variable costs can result in different contribution margins. As a consequence, break-even points can change, depending on the sales mix, or proportions of the products sold. An assumption in break-even analysis for a multiproduct business is that the sales mix will not change during the planning period. If the sales mix does change, the break-even point will also change.

REPAIR

- Reduce long-term debts.
- Refinance debts at low interest rates.
- Cut down discretionary fixed costs, such as advertising, research and development, training, and public relations costs.
- Trim down the labor force.
- Downsize operations and sell off marginal assets and profit centers.

---

* $0.6 \times$ before-tax profit = after-tax profit

   $0.6 \times$ before-tax profit = $240,000

$$\text{Before-tax profit} = \frac{\$240,000}{0.6} = \$400,000$$

- Reduce variable costs.
- Find less costly combinations of input materials.
- Develop Just-in-Time (JIT) techniques for reducing the break-even point.
- Improve the efficiency of the production line by reducing the labor cost required to manufacture the product.

PREVENTION TECHNIQUES

- Tightly control all costs.
- Use surplus funds to pay off or reduce the debt.
- Use statistical cost control charts to ensure that the cost stays within a normal (tolerable) range.
- Introduce new products with a JIT format.
- Reconfirm the break-even point of the product before it enters the market.

SPILLOVER EFFECTS. A continuous deterioration in profits would lower the market value of the company. When a product or service does not break even, it generates losses, and in the long run the company may be forced to shut down. Even if the company survives, its failure to break even will prevent it from introducing a new product or service, modernizing its facilities, or heading off production and administrative problems.

See also EXCESSIVE OPERATING LEVERAGE and UNREALISTIC BREAK-EVEN POINT.

Problem: Excessive Cost-to-Production Volume

IDENTIFYING SYMPTOMS

- Sales result in low or no profits even if all the items produced are sold at a fair market price.
- As production volume increases, so does loss.
- The product does not show a profit at the expected break-even point.

CAUSES

- The production volume is too low or too high. If actual production is below the optimal level, then opportunity cost (the cost of not producing more to make additional profits) is added to the total manufacturing cost; hence the cost for the production volume would be too high. If actual production volume is too high, then excess production is not sold and becomes a *sunk cost* that increases total manufacturing cost. (A sunk cost is one incurred in the past whose total will not be affected by any decision made now or in the future.) The result is that the cost for the production volume will be too high.

- Inability to control or cut down on costs.

- Failure to understand the relationship between a cost and production volume.

- Lack of a cost-control system, such as the use of variance analysis (comparing actual cost to standard cost) and statistical cost control.

- An unrealistic break-even point was calculated in early production runs.

- The cost associated with the product has increased since the original value was calculated.

- Yields of the product are lower than predicted (increased cost).

MEASUREMENT AND ANALYSIS

- Use the contribution margin ratio (contribution margin/sales) to help determine whether or not the variable cost is too high. Compare the ratio with the industry average to make such a decision, and perform a contribution analysis. *See* LOWERED PRICES SHRINK MARGINS in Chapter 11.

- Use earnings before interest and taxes (EBIT) over sales ratio to determine whether fixed cost is too high for the production volume, assuming the contribution margin is at a normal level.

- Plot costs over time to see if they are out of the ordinary. Examine the trend in the relationship between the cost and volume.

- Measure unit cost for each product affected. If the value is higher than initially targeted, check production problems.

- Measure the yields of the product. The yields should be at or above predetermined values to meet cost projection.

- Determine productivity and efficiency by department.

REPAIR

- Reduce operating costs.

- Identify desired levels of productivity and efficiency by department or unit.

- Cut nonessential expenditures, not vital operating costs. Some possible solutions in each area follow.

Payroll

- Look for overstaffing in every functional area.
- Reduce excess personnel and those performing below satisfactory levels.

Manufacturing

- Incorporate computer-aided product design and manufacturing.
- Reduce high levels of scrap, defective work, rework, and customer returns.
- Consider using Just-in-Time (JIT) inventory planning.
- Investigate idle labor and machine breakdown.
- Establish employee training programs to increase worker productivity.
- Reduce the cycle time for production. A reduction in cycle time reduces the work-in-process (WIP) and the costs that must be maintained.

PREVENTION TECHNIQUES

- Develop a schedule showing the different capacity levels at which the firm can produce items.
- Develop an accurate cost function for producing each item.
- Develop a good equilibrium price. This, together with an accurate analysis of both production capacity and costs, will help determine the number of units that need to be produced to generate the most profits.
- Institute techniques to lower cost before starting production.
- Go over the variable cost function again before start-up to determine the validity of the variable cost selected.

SPILLOVER EFFECTS. Excessive costs relative to manufacturing volume may result in planning and scheduling inefficiencies, cancellation of contracts, and reduction of staff. Excessive cost-to-production-volume leads to high opportunity and sunk costs that can end in lower or no profits. As a result, the earnings per share will go down, and hence the price of the stock will decrease. The company may also be subject to a lower issuance price for its bond offerings, resulting in a higher cost of financing to compensate for the increased risk of lower profits. An increase in selling prices to recoup losses may cause a loss of business.

See also COSTS NOT CLOSELY TRACKED, DISTORTED COST INFORMATION, EXCES-

SIVE LABOR COSTS, INADEQUATE COST CONTROLS, PRODUCT OR SERVICE DOES NOT BREAK EVEN, and UNREALISTIC BREAK-EVEN POINT.

Problem: Weak Sales Mix

IDENTIFYING SYMPTOMS

- Sales mix does not occur as budgeted.
- Lower-priced sales items are sold at a disproportionately high rate as compared to the higher-priced, higher-margin items.
- There is an excessive inventory of one product.
- Costs are higher than originally budgeted.

CAUSES

- It is often easier to sell lower-margin, and hence, cheaper, items than top-of-the-line models.
- The sales quotas are often set in number of units to be sold rather than in profits to be made.
- There is a shift in sales mix toward a less profitable product line.
- The cost of a product increases above its projected resale value.

MEASUREMENT AND ANALYSIS.   Compute the profitability for each product.

Example: Assume that Dante, Inc. is a producer of recreational equipment. It expects to produce and sell three types of sleeping bags: the Economy, the Regular, and the Backpacker. Information on the bags is given below:

| | Amounts budgeted | | | |
	Economy	Regular	Backpacker	Total
Sales	$30,000	$60,000	$10,000	$100,000
Sales mix	30%	60%	10%	100%
Less: Variable costs (VC)	24,000	40,000	5,000	69,000
Contribution margin (CM)	$6,000	$20,000	$5,000	$31,000
CM ratio	20%	$33^{1}/_3$%	50%	31%
Fixed costs				$18,600
Net income				$12,400

Assume that total sales was achieved at $100,000 but that an actual mix came out differently from the budgeted mix (i.e., for Regular, 60 percent to 30 percent and for Backpacker, 10 percent to 40 percent).

	Actual expenditure			
	Economy	Regular	Backpacker	Total
Sales	$55,000	$40,000	$5,000	$100,000
Sales mix	55%	40%	5%	100%
Less: Variable costs (VC)	44,000	26,667*	2,500†	73,167
Contribution margin (CM)	$11,000	$13,333	$2,500	$ 26,833
CM ratio	20%	33⅓%	50%	26.83%
Fixed costs				$ 18,600
Net income				$ 8,233

*$26,667 = $40,000 × (100% − 33⅓%) = $40,000 × 66⅔%
†$2,500 = $5,000 × (100% − 50%) = $5,000 × 50%

Note: The shift in sales mix toward the less profitable Economy line has caused the CM ratio for the company as a whole to drop from 31 percent to 26.83 percent. The deterioration (improvement) in the mix caused net income to go down (up).

It is important to note that generally, the shift of emphasis from low-margin products to high-margin ones will increase the overall profits of the company.

REPAIR

- Reduce the price of slow-moving products to make them more price competitive.

- Increase advertising of slow-moving products to help reduce their inventory.

- Increase advertising of higher-margin products to encourage their sales and increase profits.

Many product lines include a lower-margin price leader model and a high-margin deluxe model. To increase overall profitability, management might want to emphasize the higher-margin expensive items, but the sales force might find it easier to sell the lower-margin, cheaper models. Thus, a salesperson might meet the unit sales quota with each item at its budgeted price, but because of mix shifts, could be far short of contributing his or her share of budgeted profit.

Management should realize that greater proportions of more profitable products mean higher profits, and higher proportions of lower-margin sales reduce overall profit despite the increase in overall sales volume. Thus an unfavorable mix may easily offset a favorable increase in volume, and vice versa.

PREVENTION TECHNIQUES

- Provide more incentive to the sales force to sell higher CM lines by establishing profit quotas rather than quotas of units sold.

- Price the products at a competitive price.

- Advertise the products early in the production program to create a strong market for the products.

- Create a need for the product in the market. (An example of this approach is Intel's handling of its computer chips. The company heavily markets its new 486 chip, a higher-margin product, and only very minimally markets its older 286 chip, a lower-margin product.)

SPILLOVER EFFECTS.   Insufficient sales of high CM lines in favor of lower-margin items will lead to a buildup of higher-cost finished goods inventory (for a manufacturer), a need for a higher number of units sold with increasing marketing costs, and a shift in production mix toward lower-margin items. A poor sales mix may ultimately result in the loss of revenue and decline in profitability. There could even be a temporary stoppage of production for the product, resulting in excessive inventory. Such a shutdown might necessitate the layoff of employees until production resumes.

See also REVENUE BASE EROSION.

Problem: Unprofitable Profit Centers

IDENTIFYING SYMPTOM.   A profit center (a segment of a business whose evaluation is based on the profit it earns) generates a financial loss each month.

CAUSES

- A particular segment, or group of segments, of a firm is failing to generate sufficient contribution margin to cover direct fixed costs plus allocated common fixed costs.

- In a transfer-pricing situation, the selling division does not receive enough credit for its transfer of goods and services to the buying division. The transfer price tends to reduce the actual positive operating performance of the selling division. (A transfer price is the price charged by one department for an internal transfer of an assembled product or service to another department.)

MEASUREMENT AND ANALYSIS.   Segmental reporting (financial performance by department), based on the contribution approach, is necessary. A typical format for a contribution-margin report evaluating the performance of the division and its manager is presented below.

Contribution Margin Income Statement for Segmental Performance Evaluation

Sales

Less.   Variable production cost of sales

Equals.   Manufacturing contribution margin

Less. Variable selling and administrative expenses

Equals. Contribution margin

Less. Controllable fixed costs (e.g., salesperson salaries)

Equals. Controllable contribution margin by manager (which measures the performance of the segment manager)

Less. Uncontrollable fixed costs (e.g., depreciation, property taxes, insurance)

Equals. Segment contribution margin (measures performance of the division)

Less. Unallocated costs to divisions (which are excessively difficult to allocate objectively or are illogical to allocate, such as the president's salary, corporate research)

Equals. Income before taxes (which measures performance of the company in its entirety)

This contribution reporting is based on the following assumptions:

1. Fixed costs are much less controllable than variable costs.

2. Direct fixed costs and *common* fixed costs must be clearly distinguished. Direct fixed costs are those fixed costs that can be identified directly with a particular segment of an organization, whereas common fixed costs are those costs that cannot be identified directly with the segment. They apply to the company as a whole.

3. Common fixed costs should be clearly identified as unallocated in the contribution income statement by segments. Any attempt to allocate these types of costs, on some arbitrary basis, to the segments of the organization can destroy the value of responsibility accounting. It would lead to unfair evaluation of performance and misleading managerial decisions.

Note that the following concepts are highlighted in the contribution approach:

1. Contribution margin equals sales minus variable costs.

2. Segment margin equals contribution margin minus direct (traceable) fixed costs. Direct fixed costs include discretionary fixed costs, such as certain advertising, research and development; sales promotion; and engineering, traceable, and committed fixed costs, such as depreciation, property taxes, insurance, and the segment managers' salaries.

3. Net income equals segment margin less unallocated common fixed costs. Segmental reporting can be made by division, product or product line, sales territory, service center, salesperson, store or branch office, and domestic or foreign operation.

The segment margin is the best measure of the profitability of a segment. Unallocated fixed costs are common to the segments being evaluated and should be left unallocated in order not to distort the performance results of segments.

When the profit center is a product or service, it is important to analyze operating performance to determine if the product should be kept or dropped. Again, the contribution approach can be utilized, as illustrated in the example below.

The decision about whether or not to drop a product line must take into account both qualitative and quantitative factors. However, any final decision should be based primarily on the impact the decision will have on contribution margin or net income.

Example: Tasty Food Corporation has three major product lines: produce, meats, and canned food. The company is considering the decision to drop the meat line because the income statement shows that it is being sold at a loss. Note the income statement for these product lines, as shown in the following table.

	Produce	Meats	Canned food	Total
Sales	$10,000	$15,000	$25,000	$50,000
Less variable costs	6,000	8,000	12,000	26,000
Contribution margin	$4,000	$7,000	$13,000	$24,000
Less fixed costs				
Direct	$2,000	$6,500	$4,000	$12,500
Allocated	1,000	1,500	2,500	5,000
Total	$3,000	$8,000	$6,500	$17,500
Net income	$1,000	$(1,000)	$6,500	$6,500

In this example, direct fixed costs are those costs that are identified directly with each of the product lines, whereas allocated fixed costs are the amount of common fixed costs allocated to the product lines using some base such as space occupied. The amount of common fixed costs typically continues, regardless of the decision, and thus cannot be saved by dropping the product line to which it is distributed.

The comparative approach showing the effects on the company as a whole with and without the meat line is shown in the following table.

	Keep meats	Drop meats	Difference
Sales	$50,000	$35,000	$(15,000)
Less variable cost	26,000	18,000	(8,000)
Contribution margin	$24,000	$17,000	$(7,000)
Less fixed cost			
Direct	$12,500	$6,000	$(6,500)
Allocated	5,000	5,000	—
Total	$17,500	$11,000	$(6,500)
Net income	$6,500	$6,000	$(500)

From the table, we see that by dropping meats the company will lose an additional $500. Therefore, the meat product line should be kept. One of the great dangers in allocating common fixed costs is that such allocations can make a product line look less profitable than it really is. Because of such an allocation, the meat line showed a loss of $1000, but it in effect contributes $500 ($7000 − $6500) to the recovery of the company's common fixed costs.

All arbitrary allocations of overhead should be ignored while evaluating a segment's performance. In deciding whether to discontinue operations, it is necessary to consider the direct (removable) fixed costs, the contribution margin, and the overall effect on the firm's profitability.

REPAIR. Sell or liquidate the unprofitable profit centers if the contribution margin is negative. A "what if" analysis is required to ascertain whether the divestiture of such a segment would improve the performance of the firm as a whole.

PREVENTION TECHNIQUES. Reorganize the profit center to provide for stronger management to improve cost and yields.

SPILLOVER EFFECTS. Depending on the extent of the loss, retaining unprofitable profit centers can drive down profits or maintain a higher level of profit (if contribution margin is positive). Staff may have to be reduced to cut costs. The elimination of the product from the product line may cause customers for the other products to find an alternate supplier resulting in lost business for the company. The failure to eliminate or correct unprofitable business segments may ultimately result in lower credit ratings, decline in the market price of the issuing company's stocks and bonds, and in severe cases, insolvency and bankruptcy.

See also LACK OF RESIDUAL INCOME, LOW RATE OF RETURN, LACK OF COST INFORMATION, EXCESSIVE LABOR COSTS, INABILITY TO CURB FINANCIAL PROBLEMS, and ACTUAL COSTS EXCEED BUDGETED COSTS.

Problem: Potential Loss of a Contract

IDENTIFYING SYMPTOMS

- Friction between company and client.
- Disagreements over such issues as pricing, quality, and timely delivery.
- Purchasers refuse to pay and contemplate lawsuits for breach of contract.
- Competitors offer to sell or produce the merchandise or service contracted for at a lower price.

CAUSES

- The company cannot manufacture the product or deliver the service because it lacks expertise or has labor problems.

- Government contracts are uncertain because of cuts in spending and changes in priorities.

- Prices have not been correctly computed.

- Quality control is poor.

- Purchase and delivery commitments made to clients cannot be met.

- Poor economic conditions lead to order cancellations.

- Other companies offer tough competition for the contract.

- Management lacks the facilities or expertise to produce and deliver the product or service.

MEASUREMENT AND ANALYSIS.   Pricing policies using contribution margin analysis may be helpful in contract negotiations for a product or service. Often such business is sought during the slack season, when it may be financially beneficial to bid on extra business at a competitive price that covers all variable costs and makes some contribution to fixed costs plus profits. Knowledge of a company's variable and fixed costs is necessary to make an accurate bid price determination.

REPAIR

- Determine the bid price to charge on a contract using relevant costing (costs relevant to a decision) when idle capacity arises. At idle capacity, total fixed costs are irrelevant to pricing a contract. A contract may appear to be a loss because total costs (fixed and variable) exceed total revenue. However, the contract should be accepted as long as there is a contribution margin (total revenue exceeds variable cost) because additional profit is earned since the incremental fixed costs are zero.

- Subcontract the work to other contractors if management feels it lacks the proper production facilities or expertise to produce and deliver the product or service.

See LOWERED PRICES SHRINK MARGINS in Chapter 11 for a full discussion.

PREVENTION TECHNIQUES

- Expand inspection efforts during production to assure that the product meets quality standards.

- Approve overtime and expand the staff to assure that the product or service is delivered on time.

- Keep the client up-to-date about unexpected, unavoidable bottle-necks.

- Discuss any production or financial problems with the client in a friendly manner and make appropriate compromises.

- Engage in joint ventures with other companies to share possible risks.

- Establish a public relations program to protect current business and attract new business by emphasizing the positive attributes (reliability, integrity, quality of product or services) of the company. (In this context, a change in name may enable a company to divorce itself from its old negative reputation.)

- Examine all future contracts to ensure that the company does not overestimate its ability to deliver a product or service.

SPILLOVER EFFECTS.   A loss of contracts means a decline in revenue, profitability, and cash flow. Layoffs may be necessary, along with other cost reduction programs to save costs. Other sources of business reliant on those contracts may be lost. The company may be perceived by other clients as having problems and may shift their business to competitors.

See also EXCESSIVE LABOR COSTS and PRODUCT OR SERVICE DOES NOT BREAK EVEN.

Problem: Product Refinement Generates a Loss

IDENTIFYING SYMPTOM.   Falling sales and/or profit margin.

CAUSES.   The loss in sales and/or profit margin may arise from:

- Cost overruns.
- Inaccurate pricing.
- Ineffective advertising.
- An overoptimistic estimate of demand for the product.

This may be the result of:

- Inadequate planning.
- Deficient engineering.
- Misstatement of cost estimates.
- Lack of product quality.
- Quantity of product offered at a given price.

- Production inefficiencies.
- Poor worker performance.

MEASUREMENT AND ANALYSIS

- Compare sales and profit before and after product refinement.
- Compare budgeted costs to actual costs.
- Analyze the change in product demand.

REPAIR.   Determine whether data on direct labor and material costs are accurate. Management can then stop production, immediately increase the retail price of the product, or implement a cost-cutting program. Streamline the manufacturing process by changing plant layout.

PREVENTION TECHNIQUES

- Plan carefully before refining the product.
- Separate all factory and corporate support systems and trace them to individual products being offered for sale.
- Reduce the costs of logistics, production, marketing and sales, distribution, product services, technology, financial and general administration.
- Make the accounting department provide realistic cost figures arising from the change.
- Train workers in the modified product.
- Use customer surveys to determine whether there is a demand for the proposed refined product.
- Test-market the product before it is introduced.
- Set up a separate company with a different name to protect the parent company from failure.
- Increase product liability insurance against possible consumer lawsuits based on the negligent manufacture of the product.

SPILLOVER EFFECTS.   A refined product that is not profitable will result in lower earnings and higher customer dissatisfaction that can cost the firm future sales. The product may also generate government investigation because of possible deceptive practices.

Chapter

5

Anemic Financial Statements

A business that fails to maintain adequate liquid assets cannot pay its obligations when due. This may lead to insolvency and possible bankruptcy. A company that owes more than it owns is in a very precarious financial situation. Its credit rating will deteriorate, resulting in less available funds, higher costs of financing, lower market price for its stocks and bonds, and greater loan restrictions. Suppliers will be reluctant to grant credit.

If assets are not efficiently used or turned over, profit margins will deteriorate and obsolescence may occur. A business can only contract when it is earning a low rate of return on invested capital (total assets). High-risk assets cannot easily be sold to generate sufficient cash.

A declining trend in earnings, coupled with low-quality income statement elements should raise a red flag of warning. Poor earnings quality will result in a lower price-earnings ratio, lower bond rating, and excessive debt restrictions. Unstable operations mean uncertainty and risk to investors, creditors, and suppliers. It is difficult to reliably predict future results when an inconsistent trend in revenue and earnings exists.

Problem: Inadequate Working Capital

IDENTIFYING SYMPTOMS

- A lack of current funds sufficient to meet current obligations
- Difficulty collecting notes and accounts receivable, converting short-term investments into cash, and obtaining credit from suppliers

CAUSES

- Working capital is inadequate because the company is engaged in capital expansion or is highly capital intensive.
- A lack of cash flow from operations results in insufficient liquid assets.

- The company is financing its noncurrent assets with short-term debt, a questionable financing strategy because the debt will have to be paid back before cash is received from the sale of its fixed assets.

MEASUREMENT AND ANALYSIS. Working capital equals the excess of total current assets over total current liabilities and is a measure of a company's short-term liquidity. It is a margin of safety available for meeting the cash demands of the operating cycle of a business.

The trade-off between return and risk must be considered. If funds move from fixed assets (e.g., plant and equipment) to current assets (e.g., inventory) there will be a reduction in liquidity risk, greater ability to obtain short-term financing, and greater financial flexibility, because the business can better adjust current assets to changes in sales volume. However, the return on current assets is usually less than the return on fixed assets. The longer it takes to manufacture goods or to resell purchased goods, the greater the demand for working capital.

REPAIR. Additional working capital can be generated by increasing current assets and decreasing current liabilities. Therefore, money should be invested in current assets rather than in fixed assets. Financing should be in the form of long-term obligations rather than short-term debt.

PREVENTION TECHNIQUES

- Finance the purchase of fixed assets with long-term debt.
- Borrow funds using long-term obligations and retain the funds in cash or other current assets.

SPILLOVER EFFECTS. A poor working capital position means that the company is less liquid. This can result in higher financing costs and an inability to obtain financing.

See also INADEQUATE LIQUIDITY and INADEQUATE CASH POSITION.

Problem: Inadequate Liquidity

IDENTIFYING SYMPTOMS

- Failure to pay bills or other debt payments on time
- Inability to buy inventory or assets
- Failure to obtain financing

- Lower profitability
- Inability to take cash discounts by making early payment
- A deteriorating credit rating
- Difficulty obtaining loans on favorable terms

CAUSES

- Failure to expedite the collection of accounts receivable and to reduce the lag between the time customers pay their bills and the time the checks are converted into cash
- Overspending
- Excessive debt
- Poor management of current assets (cash, accounts receivable, and inventory)
- Failure to properly assess risk

MEASUREMENT AND ANALYSIS.   Numerous measures exist to evaluate a company's liquidity, including the following ratios and computations:

- *Current ratio* (current assets/current liabilities) and *quick ratio* (cash plus marketable securities plus accounts receivable/current liabilities). High ratios are needed when a company has difficulty borrowing on short notice. NOTE: Current assets that are pledged to secure long-term liabilities are not available to meet current debt.
- *Accounts receivable turnover* (credit sales/average accounts receivable) and *collection period* (360/accounts receivable turnover). The accounts receivable turnover gives the number of times receivables are collected during the year. The higher the turnover the better, since this means the company is collecting quickly from customers. However, an excessively high turnover might indicate that the company's credit policy is too stringent, with the company not tapping the potential for profit through sales to customers in higher-risk classes. The collection period indicates how long it takes to collect from customers. A long collection period indicates a danger that customer balances may become uncollectible. Compare the collection period to the due date. Prepare an aging schedule. However, a longer collection period may be justified, such as when the business extends the credit terms in connection with the introduction of a new product.
- *Inventory turnover* (cost of goods sold/average inventory) and *age of inventory* (360 days/inventory turnover). The inventory

turnover reveals how many times inventory is sold during the year. A decline in the turnover rate indicates a buildup of inventory, overestimating sales, a lack of balance in inventory, or deficiencies in the product line or marketing effort. However, a low turnover may be appropriate in some cases, such as when higher inventory levels occur in anticipation of rapidly rising prices (as in the case of oil). A high turnover rate may indicate inadequate inventory levels, which may lead to a loss in business. The age of the inventory is the number of days it is held prior to its sale. If the holding period increases, there is the risk of inability to sell the asset and possible obsolescence. If the holding period decreases, it may represent underinvestment in inventory that can cause deficient customer service and lost sales.

- *Operating cycle* is the number of days from cash to inventory to accounts receivable to cash. The operating cycle equals the collection period on accounts receivable plus the age of inventory. It reveals how long cash is tied up in receivables and inventory. A long operating cycle means cash is less available to meet short-term obligations.

- *Working capital* is the liquid reserve available to satisfy contingencies and uncertainties. It is the excess of current assets over current liabilities. A high working capital balance is mandated if the business is unable to borrow on short notice.

- *Sales to current assets.*   A high turnover rate indicates deficient working capital. Current liabilities may be due and payable before inventories and receivables can be converted into cash.

- *Working capital provided from net income.*   A company's liquid position is improved when net profits result in liquid funds.

- *Working capital provided from operations to total liabilities* indicates the degree to which internally generated working capital cash flow is available to satisfy obligations.

- *Cash plus marketable securities to current liabilities* shows the immediate amount of cash available to satisfy short-term debt.

- *Cash plus marketable securities to working capital.*   A low ratio means less protection to short-term creditors in meeting debt shortly coming due.

- *Cost of sales, operating expenses, and taxes to average total current assets.*   The trend in this ratio is used to analyze the adequacy of current assets to satisfy ongoing business-related expenses.

- *Quick assets to the year's cash expenses* indicates the number of days of total operating expenses that highly liquid assets could support.

- *The ratios of fixed assets to short-term debt and short-term debt to long-term debt* can indicate dangerous financial policies. If an entity finances long-term assets with short-term obligations, it may have a problem meeting the payments when due, because the return and proceeds from the fixed assets will not be realized before the maturity dates of the current obligations. The business will be vulnerable in a money-market squeeze.

- *Accounts payable to average daily purchases* reveals the number of days it takes for the business to pay creditors. It measures the extent to which accounts payable represent current obligations rather than overdue obligations.

- *Current liabilities to total liabilities and current liabilities to non-current liabilities.*   Higher ratios mean less liquidity because there is a greater proportion of total debt that must be paid shortly.

- *Defensive interval ratio* indicates how long the business can operate on its liquid assets without needing revenues from next period's sources. It reveals corporate near-term liquidity as a basis to meet expenditures.

- *Liquidity index* indicates the number of days during which assets are removed from cash. It is computed as follows:

	Amount	×	Days Away from Cash =	Total
Cash	$20,000	×	—	—
Accounts receivable	50,000	×	30	$1,500,000
Inventory	80,000	×	50	4,000,000
	$150,000			$5,500,000

$$\text{Index} = \frac{\$5,500,000}{\$150,000}$$

$$= 36.7 \text{ days}$$

- A company's liquidity ratios must be compared with industry norms and ratios of major competitors to obtain a relative standing.

REPAIR

- Expedite the collection of cash by reducing the lag between the time that customers receive their bills and actual payment.
- Slow disbursements so that the company can continue to receive the use of the cash.
- Convert investments into cash.
- Sell unprofitable operating divisions and subsidiaries.
- Open new credit lines.

PREVENTION TECHNIQUES

- Curb expenditures.
- Limit excessive debt.
- Obtain lines of credit with financing institutions.
- Issue stocks and/or bonds.
- Restrict capital expansion.
- Slow cash disbursements to pay only impending obligations and invest excess funds.

SPILLOVER EFFECTS

- Inability to obtain short-term financing
- Failure to meet short-term payments
- Lower credit ratings
- Decline in the market price of the company's stocks and bonds
- Financial inability to make profitable investments
- Possible insolvency and bankruptcy

See also BANKRUPTCY LOOMS, EXCESSIVE DEBT, INADEQUATE WORKING CAPITAL, and INSOLVENCY.

Problem: Insolvency

IDENTIFYING SYMPTOMS.   An insolvent business cannot satisfy its short- and long-term obligations and interest payments as they mature. This may be due to high fixed interest costs, coupled with excessive debt. There is also high realization risk in noncurrent assets.

CAUSES

- Poor operating performance
- Deficient cash flow
- Liabilities in excess of the company's ability to pay
- Debt incurred to prevent a hostile takeover
- Managerial incompetence

MEASUREMENT AND ANALYSIS.   A company may be technically insolvent, even though its assets exceed its liabilities, when it lacks sufficient liquid assets to pay maturing debts. The term "bankruptcy" indicates that the company's liabilities exceed its assets. Under the law, either technical insolvency or bankruptcy is characterized as the financial failure of the company. Solvency ratios must be studied and compared to industry averages. Some useful ratios follow.

- *Total liabilities to stockholders' equity* (commonly referred to as debt/equity ratio, financial leverage). High leverage has risk because it may be difficult for the company to pay interest and principal while trying to obtain additional financing. The usefulness of the ratio is also enhanced if securities are valued at their year-end market value rather than at book value.

- *Long-term debt to stockholders' equity.* A higher ratio is unfavorable because of the risk in repaying long-term obligations.

- *Total liabilities to total assets* (commonly referred to as debt ratio). A high ratio is unfavorable because the company is already overburdened with debt.

- *Cash flow to long-term debt* appraises the adequacy of available funds to pay noncurrent obligations.

- *Net income before taxes and interest to interest* reflects the number of times interest expense is covered. It reveals the magnitude of the decline in income that a firm can absorb and still meet its interest payment obligations.

- *Cash flow generated from operations plus interest to interest* indicates the cash actually available to the business to meet interest charges, since cash and not net income is used to pay interest.

- *Net income before taxes and fixed charges to fixed charges* measures a company's ability to meet fixed costs. The ratio indicates the risk involved when business activity falls and a company is in danger of being unable to pay its fixed charges (e.g., rent, insurance, interest).

- *Cash flow provided from operations plus fixed charges to fixed charges* indicates the available cash to pay fixed charges.

- *Noncurrent assets to noncurrent liabilities.* Long-term debt will ultimately be paid out of long-term assets. A high ratio indicates protection for long-term creditors.

- *Retained earnings to total assets* reveals a company's profitability over the years.

REPAIR

- Sell marginal (nonprofitable) assets.
- Close marginal stores.

- Restructure cash collection policies for credit sales.
- Obtain new credit lines.
- Sell corporate stock.
- Lengthen payment dates on obligations.
- Lay off employees.

PREVENTION TECHNIQUES

- Obtain additional financing from equity sources, such as the sale of preferred and common stock.
- Develop open lines of credit.
- Have short payback periods on projects.
- Adjust quickly to changes in business conditions.
- Change the amount and timing of future cash flows to adjust to sudden developments.
- Downsize.
- Restructure.
- Practice conservative financial management.

SPILLOVER EFFECTS.   Potential creditors are reluctant to give financing to a company with a high debt position. If they do, interest rates will be higher. A company that cannot pay its creditors will be unable to operate effectively and profitably. It may face eventual bankruptcy.

See also BANKRUPTCY LOOMS, EXCESSIVE DEBT, and INADEQUATE LIQUIDITY.

Problem: Excessive Debt

IDENTIFYING SYMPTOMS

- Cash flow problems
- Loan restrictions
- Lower credit rating
- Inability to meet interest and principal payments on maturing debt
- Increased financing costs

CAUSES

- Interest and principal payment obligations are set by contract and must be met, regardless of the firm's economic position.

- Excessive debt is incurred to finance expansion or prevent a hostile takeover.

- A decline in profitability forces the company to borrow externally to finance normal operations.

- The business cannot issue additional shares of stock because prospective investors view it as a poor risk; it has to issue debt securities or use lines of credit.

- Management has failed to realistically forecast business needs and cash flow.

- The company has not exercised fiscal self-control.

- Executives have failed to appreciate that growth at any cost may be too expensive.

MEASUREMENT AND ANALYSIS.   Examine the trend in the following ratios over the last five years:

- *Total debt to total stockholders' equity.*   A higher ratio means more debt and risk.

- *Noncurrent assets to noncurrent liabilities.*   A lower ratio means fewer fixed assets available to meet long-term debt.

- *Short-term debt to long-term debt.*   A higher ratio means less liquidity because more debt is coming due in the short term.

- *Current liabilities to sales.*   Short-term debt may be stretched to support sales growth.

- *Short-term debt to total liabilities.*   A high ratio points to less liquidity.

- *Net income plus interest divided by interest.*   A lower ratio means less earnings available to meet interest payments.

- *Sales to accounts payable.*   A high ratio indicates the inability to obtain short-term credit in the form of cost-free funds to finance sales growth.

In appraising current liabilities, management must determine which of the liabilities are "pressing" and which are "patient." Patient liabilities (e.g., suppliers) are more tolerant and may allow delayed payment or even adjust the amounts owed in times of financial difficulties. Pressing obligations, however, must be paid on time. These obligations include taxes and salaries. Examine the trend in the relationship of pressing liabilities to patient liabilities. An increasing trend reflects greater liquidity risk.

Example: Company C reports the following data:

	19X1	19X2
Current Liabilities		
Accounts payable	$30,000	$26,000
Short-term loans payable	50,000	80,000
Commercial paper	40,000	60,000
Total current liabilities	$120,000	$166,000
Total noncurrent liabilities	300,000	302,000
Total liabilities	$420,000	$468,000
Sales	$1,000,000	$1,030,000

Relevant ratios follow:

Current liabilities to total liabilities	28.6%	35.5%
Current liabilities to sales	12.0%	16.1%
Pressing current liabilities to patient current liabilities (short-term loans payable plus commercial paper/accounts payable)	3.0	5.4

Company C has greater liquidity risk in 19X2, as indicated by the higher ratios of current liabilities to total liabilities, current liabilities to sales, and pressing current liabilities to patient current liabilities.

Consider off-balance-sheet liabilities that are not reported in the body of the financial statements but may require future payment or services, such as litigation, lease commitment, and cosigning a loan.

REPAIR

- Extend the maturity dates on loans.
- Renegotiate with lenders to lower the interest rate on loans.
- Defer the payment of loans for one year.
- Offer creditors the opportunity to convert their credit holdings into stock of the corporation at a favorable conversion rate.
- Issue common stock and preferred stock at a favorable price to provide equity funds so as to improve the mix in the capital structure by lowering the debt to equity ratio.
- Sell assets to meet debt payments.
- Assign accounts receivable.

PREVENTION TECHNIQUES

- Establish a maximum debt ceiling for the company that cannot be exceeded in any case.

- Institute a policy whereby assets are to be purchased only when operations absolutely require their acquisition.

- Negotiate open lines of credit to assure that funds will be available when needed.

- Review loan provisions, such as acceleration clauses stipulating that the loan is immediately due if an installment payment is missed or the debt/equity ratio increases above a specified percentage. Compare existing terms of debt versus the company's actual financial status to ascertain the degree to which the current position exceeds the compliance requirement.

- Use spontaneous sources of financing, because they result from typical operating activities. They are essentially interest-free funds and should be extended to their maximum. Included are accounts payable and accrued expenses.

- If the company is a seasonal business that is a net borrower, use more long-term financing as a precautionary measure.

- Arrange to have the company's debts mature during its profitable season rather than during a period of slow sales.

- Do not incur debt when the return earned on borrowed funds is less than the after-tax cost of that debt.

- Issue lower-cost debt, such as commercial paper.

- Avoid making unrealistic promises about future earnings and profitability. If the financial projection is conservative, a bank or financing institution is more likely to believe the company and extend credit on favorable terms.

- Issue stock dividends in lieu of cash dividends, so that cash is available to meet debt obligations.

- Establish a sinking fund where payments are made each period to retire debt at maturity.

SPILLOVER EFFECTS.   If debt is excessive, the interest rate on further debt financing will be higher because of the greater risk, and additional financing may be unavailable. If the business cannot meet its debt payments, it may be forced into bankruptcy. Excessive interest and principal payment obligations may alter dividend policy by requiring the omission of one or more periodic dividend payments. This will have a negative impact on the market price of the company's outstanding shares and subsequent public offerings.

See also INADEQUATE LIQUIDITY and INSOLVENCY.

Problem: Off-Balance-Sheet Liabilities

IDENTIFYING SYMPTOM.   Prospective liabilities are not reported on the balance sheet.

CAUSE.   Future obligations. For example, guarantees of future performance and postretirement benefits may involve considerable future expenditures.

MEASUREMENT AND ANALYSIS.   Off-balance-sheet financing is an attempt to generate monies by borrowing money without having to record the liability on the financial statements. The dollar amount of an off-balance-sheet liability must be determined and considered a future drain on corporate financial resources.

> **Example:**   In one company's pension plan, the projected benefit obligation is $6 million, while the accumulated benefit obligation is $5 million. The projected benefit obligation is the discounted value of future pension benefit payments to retired employees based on future salaries, while the accumulated benefit obligation is the discounted value of future pension benefit payments to retired employees based on current salaries. In this case, the company has an off-balance-sheet obligation of $1 million ($6 million − $5 million).

REPAIR.   Off-balance-sheet liabilities may be funded through insurance, such as insurance against product liability.

PREVENTION TECHNIQUES

- Options and other protective provisions in lease agreements
- Avoiding agreements for future transactions
- Minimizing employee benefits

SPILLOVER EFFECTS.   The future payment of an off-balance-sheet liability will reduce a company's cash position and liquidity. If the amount is substantial, such as huge lawsuit damages not covered by insurance, the insolvency and bankruptcy of the business are possible.

Problem: Deficient Asset Use and Turnover

IDENTIFYING SYMPTOMS

- Declining sales and profits
- Idle capacity
- Breakdowns
- Low output relative to input
- Buildup in inventory and/or receivables
- Inactive use of assets

CAUSES

- Inefficient or obsolete equipment
- Multishift operations
- Temporary changes in demand
- Interruptions in the supply of raw materials and parts
- Poor production scheduling
- Inadequate supervision

MEASUREMENT AND ANALYSIS.   Asset utilization has as its ultimate measure the amount of sales generated because sales is the first and essential step to profits. *No* assets should be held unless they contribute to revenue or generate income.

Asset utilization and turnover ratios include:

- *Accounts receivable turnover.*   See INADEQUATE LIQUIDITY.
- *Inventory turnover.*   See INADEQUATE LIQUIDITY.
- *Sales to cash.*   A high turnover may indicate a cash shortage. A low turnover may reflect the holding of idle and unnecessary cash balances.
- *Sales to working capital.*   A high ratio may indicate inadequate working capital, which reflects negatively on liquidity.
- *Sales to fixed assets.*   A low ratio means inefficient utilization or obsolescence of fixed assets because they are not generating sufficient sales. There may also be excess capacity and interruptions in the supply of raw materials.
- *Sales to total assets.*   A low ratio indicates that the total assets of the business are not providing adequate revenue. A low ratio of sales to floor space of machinery indicates less efficient utilization of space.

REPAIR

- Improve asset turnover by increasing sales, reducing investment, or both.
- Use assets more efficiently or sell them.
- Be sure fixed assets are functioning properly. Repairs and maintenance are necessary to improve efficiency.
- Lease equipment if production of a new product line has an uncertain period of benefit.
- Accelerate collections.

- Computerize inventory records and order systems.
- Sell off unused or inactive assets so that the cash obtained can be used elsewhere (such as to pay debt).

PREVENTION TECHNIQUES

- Institute a regular program of overhaul or modernization.
- Compare the investment in assets to the value of the output produced. If assets are excessive, consolidate present operations, perhaps by selling some of the assets and investing the proceeds for a higher return, or using them to expand into a more profitable area.

SPILLOVER EFFECTS.   A cash shortage may result in a liquidity crisis if the business has no other available sources of funds. Inadequate utilization of capital facilities will mean lower sales and earnings. Inactive assets result in excessive costs.

See also INADEQUATE LIQUIDITY, LOW RATE OF RETURN, and POOR PROFITABILITY AND GROWTH.

Problem: Low Rate of Return

IDENTIFYING SYMPTOMS

- High management turnover.
- Lower earnings estimates issued by brokerage analysts
- Lower stock rankings published by financial newspapers and business weeklies
- A drop in bond ratings by financial advising services

CAUSES

- Declining sales
- Inability to raise prices
- Lower profit margins because of excessive costs
- Lower asset turnover

MEASUREMENT AND ANALYSIS.   Return on investment (ROI) relates net income to invested capital (total assets). It provides a standard for evaluating how efficiently financial management employs the average dollar invested in a firm's assets, whether that dollar came from owners or creditors. Furthermore, a better ROI can also translate directly into a higher return on the stockholders' equity.

In the past, financial managers have tended to focus only on the margin earned and have ignored the turnover of assets. It is important to realize that excessive funds tied up in assets can be as much of a burden on profitability as excessive expenses can. The DuPont Corporation was the first major company to recognize the importance of looking at both net profit margin and total asset turnover in assessing the performance of an organization. The ROI breakdown, known as the DuPont formula, is expressed as a product of these two factors. It is shown below.

$$\text{ROI} = \frac{\text{net profit after taxes}}{\text{total assets}} = \frac{\text{net profit after taxes}}{\text{sales}} \times \frac{\text{sales}}{\text{total assets}}$$

$$= \text{net profit margin} \times \text{total asset turnover}$$

The DuPont formula combines the income statement and balance sheet for this otherwise static measure of performance. Net profit margin measures profitability or operating efficiency. It is the percentage of profit earned on sales. This percentage shows how many cents attach to each dollar of sales. On the other hand, total asset turnover measures how well a company manages its assets. It is the number of times by which the investment in assets turns over each year to generate sales.

The breakdown of ROI is based on the thesis that the profitability of a firm is directly related to management's ability to manage assets efficiently and to control expenses effectively.

Generally, a better management performance (i.e., a high or above-average ROI) produces a higher return to equity holders. However, even a poorly managed company that suffers from a below-average performance can generate an above-average return on the stockholders' equity, simply called the return on equity (ROE). This is because borrowed funds can magnify the returns a company's profits represent to its stockholders.

Another version of the DuPont formula, called the modified DuPont formula, reflects this effect. The formula ties together the ROI and the degree of financial leverage (use of borrowed funds). The financial leverage is measured by the equity multiplier, which is the ratio of a company's total asset base to its equity investment, or, stated another way, the ratio of dollars of assets held to dollars of stockholders' equity. It is calculated by dividing total assets by stockholders' equity. This measurement indicates how much of a company's assets are financed by stockholders' equity and how much with borrowed funds.

The return on equity (ROE) is calculated as:

$$\text{ROE} = \frac{\text{net profit after taxes}}{\text{stockholders' equity}} = \frac{\text{net profit after taxes}}{\text{total assets}}$$

$$\times \frac{\text{total assets}}{\text{stockholders' equity}} = \text{ROI} \times \text{equity multiplier}$$

ROE measures the returns earned on the owners' (both preferred and common stockholders) investment. The use of the equity multiplier to convert the ROI to the ROE reflects the impact of the leverage (use of debt) on stockholders' return.

$$\text{The equity multiplier} = \frac{\text{total assets}}{\text{stockholders' equity}} = \frac{1}{(1 - \text{debt ratio})}$$

Example: Assume stockholders' equity of $45,000 and total assets of $100,000. Then,

$$\text{Equity multiplier} = \frac{\text{total assets}}{\text{stockholders' equity}} = \frac{\$100,000}{\$45,000} = 2.22$$

$$= \frac{1}{(1 - \text{debt ratio})} = \frac{1}{(1 - .55)} = \frac{1}{.45} = 2.22$$

$$\text{ROE} = \frac{\text{net profit after taxes}}{\text{stockholders' equity}} = \frac{\$18,000}{\$45,000} = 40\%$$

$$= \text{ROI} \times \text{equity multiplier} = 18\% \times 2.22 = 40\%$$

If the company used only equity, the 18% ROI would equal ROE. However, 55 percent of the firm's capital is supplied by creditors ($45,000/$100,000 = 45 percent is the equity-to-asset ratio; $55,000/$100,000 = 55 percent is the debt ratio). Since the 18 percent ROI goes entirely to stockholders who put up only 45 percent of the capital, the ROE is higher than 18 percent. This example indicates that the company was using leverage (debt) favorably.

If the assets in which the funds are invested can earn more than the fixed rate of return required by the creditors, the leverage is positive and the common stockholders benefit. This formula enables the company to break its ROE into a profit margin portion (net profit margin), an efficiency-of-asset-utilization portion (total asset turnover), and a use-of-leverage portion (equity multiplier). It shows that the company can raise shareholder return by employing leverage—taking on more debt to help finance growth.

Since financial leverage affects net profit margin through the added interest costs, financial management must look at the various pieces of this ROE equation, within the context of the whole, to earn the highest return for stockholders. Financial managers must determine what combination of asset return and leverage will work best in its competitive environment. The relative contributions of the net profit margin and asset turnover ratio in the ROI relationship differ from industry to industry.

REPAIR.   To enhance ROI:

- Improve margin by reducing expenses, raising selling prices, or increasing sales faster than expenses.
- Improve turnover by increasing sales while holding the investment in assets relatively constant, or by reducing assets.
- Improve both.

PREVENTION TECHNIQUES.   No ROI is satisfactory for all companies. The firm's structure and size influence the rate considerably. A company with a diversified product line might have only a fair return rate when all products are pooled in the analysis. In such cases, it seems advisable to establish separate objectives for each line as well as for the total company.

Sound and successful operations must point toward the optimum combination of profits, sales, and capital employed. The combination will vary, depending on the nature of the business and its products. An industry with products tailor-made to customers' specifications will have different margins and turnover ratios compared with industries that mass-produce highly competitive consumer goods.

SPILLOVER EFFECTS

- Layoffs
- Downsizing
- Declining profitability
- Lower market price of stock and bonds
- Increased cost of financing
- Lack of financing
- Corporate insolvency and bankruptcy

See also LACK OF RESIDUAL INCOME, UNPROFITABLE PROFIT CENTERS, POOR CREDIT RATING, BOND RATING DROPS, and MARKET PRICE OF STOCK FALLS.

Problem: Lack of Residual Income

IDENTIFYING SYMPTOMS

Company.   While a business shows a net income, it is only minimally profitable or is in fact actually losing money.

Division.   A division reports a profit but is not doing as well as it seems.

CAUSES

- Poor profitability
- A high opportunity cost on the total assets employed

MEASUREMENT AND ANALYSIS

Company. The higher the ratio of residual income to net income, the better.

Residual income = net income less minimum return (cost of capital)
× total assets

A residual income that is less than reported earnings indicates a financial problem.

Example: A company's net income is $632,800; total assets are $4,600,000; and cost of capital is 13.40 percent. Residual income is arrived at as follows:

Net income =	$632,800
Less minimum return × total assets 13.40% × $4,600,000 =	616,400
Residual income =	$16,400

The ratio of residual income to net income is 2.6 percent ($16,400/$632,800). This percentage is low, indicating that the company is not earning a sufficient economic income, taking into account the opportunity cost of tying up money in the business.

An increasing trend in residual income to net income may indicate a stronger degree of profitability for the business since it is earning enough to cover its imputed cost of capital.

Residual income may be projected by division, center, or specific program to assure that the company's rate of return on alternative investments is met or improved upon by each segment of the business.

By looking at residual income, you are assured that segments are not employing corporate credit for less return than could be obtained by owning marketable securities or through investment in a different business segment.

Division. Residual income is used to measure divisional performance.

Divisional residual income = divisional net income less minimum
return × divisional total assets

The minimum return is based on the company's overall cost of financing adjusted for divisional risk.

Example: Divisional earnings are $150,000; average available total assets are $2,000,000; and the cost of capital is 9 percent.

Residual income is arrived at as follows:

Divisional net income =	$150,000
Less minimum return	
× average available total assets 9% × $2,000,000 =	180,000
Residual income =	($30,000)

Although the division has earned $150,000, it has really lost $30,000, considering the opportunity cost of tying up the assets in the division.

A target residual income may be formulated to act as the division manager's objective. The trend in residual income to total available assets should be examined in appraising divisional performance.

There are many benefits to using residual income analysis:

- The same asset may be required to earn the same return rate throughout the company, regardless of the division in which the asset is located.
- Different return rates may be employed for different types of assets, depending on riskiness.
- Different return rates may be assigned to different divisions, depending on the risk associated with those divisions.

REPAIR

- Increase profitability (e.g., through immediate cost cutting).
- Use assets more efficiently.

PREVENTION TECHNIQUES

- Obtain lower-cost alternative financing.
- Improve the productivity of resources.

SPILLOVER EFFECTS. A low or negative residual income may threaten the firm's continued financial viability and success. This is because, after considering the imputed cost of financing, the company is really losing money.

See also LOW RATE OF RETURN and UNPROFITABLE PROFIT CENTERS.

Problem: High Cash-Realization Risk in Assets

IDENTIFYING SYMPTOMS

- Management cannot convert assets into cash quickly because the assets are of questionable value.

- The assets have no separate realizable value and cannot be sold, or have low cash value and high risk.

CAUSE.   Non-liquid assets no longer have their original value.

MEASUREMENT AND ANALYSIS.   The greater the dollar frequency of a company's assets in the high-risk category, the more assets and earnings are overstated. Earnings are overstated because the assets should have been written down to recognize a decline in their value. For analytical purposes, useful ratios include the percentage of high-risk assets to total assets and to sales.

Example: Company C reports receivables of $4,000,000. Included therein are the following high-risk receivables:

Notes receivable arising from extensions of unpaid balances from delinquent customers =	$100,000
Advances to politically and economically unstable foreign governments =	200,000
High-risk receivables =	$300,000

Of the receivables reported in the balance sheet, $300,000, or 7.5 percent, are of questionable quality.

Multipurpose assets are deemed to be of higher quality than single-purpose assets because they can be converted to cash more quickly. Try to maintain market price stability in assets. If the market prices of assets fluctuate, it may be difficult to sell them.

Analysts must also consider the impact of changing government policies on the company. There is an exposure to risk for companies because of the increasing number of regulatory laws and decisions by governmental regulatory bodies.

REPAIR

- Sell low-quality assets as soon as possible, before their values diminish any further.
- Correct inventory that fails to meet governmental regulatory standards prior to its sale.
- Factor accounts receivable and purchase insurance protection on questionable assets.

PREVENTION TECHNIQUES

- Avoid high cash realization risk assets.
- Minimize expenditures for such assets as leasehold improvements.

- Do not acquire high-risk companies.
- Control work-in-process levels.
- Avoid costly startup operations.
- Refrain from moving production facilities.
- Improve credit policies.
- Reevaluate credit policies for new customers.
- Minimize operations in politically and economically unstable geographic areas.
- Avoid making low-quality investments.
- Establish a committee to evaluate and appraise the acquisition of major assets.

SPILLOVER EFFECTS.   A change in asset quality will also effect a change in profits and cash flow. The sale, discarding, or malfunctioning of one operational asset may adversely affect the profitability of the remaining related assets. If many high-risk assets exist, the company facing a cash flow problem may be unable to sell assets in an emergency to meet debt obligations.

Problem: Poor Profitability and Growth

IDENTIFYING SYMPTOMS

- Declining earnings
- A negative or minimal growth rate
- Lack of funds to remain competitive or to expand
- Erosion of sales base

CAUSES

- Low return rates on assets and sales
- Failure to control costs
- Loss in market share
- Inability to take advantage of technological advances
- Low morale and high turnover
- High degree of risk
- Uninsured asset losses
- Inexperienced management
- Failure to cope with competition

Example: A decision to build a new plant or expand into a foreign market may influence the performance of the firm over the next decade. When the decision is made to build the plant, management is usually uncertain about annual operating costs and inflows, product life, interest rates, economic conditions, and technological change. Thus a wrong decision can adversely affect the company's long-term financial status.

MEASUREMENT AND ANALYSIS. The profitability and growth rate of the business should be compared over time. Further, net income and growth should be compared to competing companies and industry norms. The following ratios should also be analyzed:

$$\text{Growth rate in retained earnings} = \frac{\text{net income} - \text{dividends}}{\text{common stockholders' equity}}$$

A lower ratio reflects a company's inability to generate internal funds, and thus it must rely on external sources, such as debt and equity.

Growth rate in earnings per share

$$= \frac{\text{EPS (end of period)} - \text{EPS (beginning of period)}}{\text{EPS (beginning of period)}}$$

$$\text{Profit margin} = \frac{\text{net income}}{\text{sales}}$$

A low profit margin means that the earnings generated from revenue is deficient, reflecting poor earning power. The profit margin provides clues to a company's pricing, cost structure, and production efficiency.

$$\text{Gross profit margin} = \frac{\text{gross profit}}{\text{sales}}$$

A lower gross profit margin indicates the business is unable to control its production costs.

$$\text{Return on investment} = \frac{\text{net income}}{\text{total assets}}$$

A low return on investment means that the earnings generated by the utilization of assets in the business is deficient.

Growth rate may be expressed in terms of a compounded annual rate equal to:

$$\text{Compounded annual rate of growth} = F_n = P \times \text{FVIF}(i, n)$$

where F_n = future value amount
$\quad\quad P$ = present value amount
$\text{FVIF}(i, n)$ = future value factor based on interest rate (i) and number of periods (n)

Solving this for FVIF, we obtain:

$$\text{FVIF}(i, n) = \frac{F_n}{P}$$

Example: Assume a company has earnings per share of $2.50 in 19XX, and 10 years later the earnings per share has increased to $3.70. The compound annual rate of growth in earnings per share is computed as follows:

$$F_{10} = \$3.70 \qquad \text{and} \qquad P = \$2.50$$

Therefore,

$$\text{FVIF}(i, 10) = \frac{\$3.70}{\$2.50} = 1.48$$

From a future value of $1 table, a FVIF of 1.48 at 10 years is at $i = 4\%$. The compound annual rate of growth is therefore 4 percent.

REPAIR

- Introduce new product lines.
- Enter into joint ventures or merge with other innovative companies.
- Diversify.
- Sell off unprofitable branches and subsidiaries.
- Replace obsolete assets.
- Obtain adequate insurance coverage for all assets.
- Increase the selling prices of products.
- Improve sales volume.
- Cut costs.
- Renegotiate union contracts and employee benefits.
- Improve manufacturing efficiency.
- Enhance return rates on assets and sales.
- Reduce risk.
- Improve worker relations.
- Redirect the sales effort to improve profit margin.
- Increase asset turnover and cash collection policies.

Selling, general, and administrative expenses are easier to control than the cost of sales because they are internal to the organization and are therefore subject to cost reduction programs.

PREVENTION TECHNIQUES

- Draw up an overall advertising and sales promotion plan to increase sales and to reduce costs.
- Implement a cost-reduction program.
- Correct problem areas.
- Use computerized reports and analyses.
- Institute cash and inventory management programs.

SPILLOVER EFFECTS. A lack of earnings and negative growth may ultimately lead to a poor cash position, creating operating, liquidity, and solvency problems. Poor earnings and growth will result in a lower market price for company stock and company bonds, a deteriorating credit rating, increased cost of financing, and a lack of available funds to support operations. If corporate earning power is at a minimum or nonexistent, it may result in business failure because the enterprise is not generating sufficient cash earnings. The company may also be targeted for a takeover.

See also DEFICIENT ASSET USE AND TURNOVER, LOW RATE OF RETURN, and POOR-QUALITY EARNINGS.

Problem: Poor-Quality Earnings

IDENTIFYING SYMPTOMS

- Lower price/earnings ratio
- Higher cost of financing
- Unavailability of suitable financing
- Higher compensating balances and security required for loan agreements
- Deterioration in the company's bond rating

CAUSES

- Unrealistic accounting policies and estimates
- Inadequate provision for the maintenance and enhancement of present and future earning power (e.g., repairs and maintenance)
- Instability in operations and earnings
- Unjustified reductions in discretionary costs, depriving the business of expenditures needed for future growth (e.g., advertising, research and development)
- Decline in profitability

- Subjective and uncertain accounting estimates associated with the recognition of revenue and expenses (the further revenue and expense recognition is from the point of cash receipt and cash payment, the less objective the transaction and the more subjective the interpretations)
- High cash-realization risk of assets
- High fixed cost structure
- Susceptibility to the business cycle
- Business risk
- Low ratio of cash earnings to net income
- Low ratio of residual income to net income
- High ratio of sales returns and allowances to sales
- Deficient return on assets
- Lack of diversification

MEASUREMENT AND ANALYSIS. *Poor-quality earnings* defines earnings that do *not* relate as reasonably as possible in the circumstances to the business operations of a company within a period of time. (E.g., the most realistic accounting alternative was *not* employed.) When two competitive companies use alternative accounting policies, the financial analyst should adjust the two net incomes to a common basis to reduce the existing diversity in accounting. Information provided in footnotes may assist in the restatement process—there may be disclosure of what the earnings effect would have been if another method of accounting (e.g., inventory method) had been used.

A weak functional relationship between sales and net income may indicate that a company is manipulating its earnings.

Example: A company's ratio of net income to sales was as follows for the period 19X1 to 19X4:

19X1	19X2	19X3	19X4
12%	3%	20%	(5%)

The above pattern indicates a weak association between net income and sales, and hence the "manipulator" status may be inferred.

Analysts can determine relevant earnings per share (EPS) by making quantitative adjustments to reported EPS, with the revised figure reflecting more realistically the earning power of a company. The conversion process will result in a higher quality-of-earnings figure.

Analysts can determine more relevant or "acceptable" quality EPS by adjusting reported EPS for low-quality items. An illustration of an adjustment process follows.

Assume a company's reported EPS of $10 includes numerous low-quality components. These items are listed below as deductions from reported EPS. (Items that must be deducted from EPS in order to arrive at an "acceptable" quality EPS were chosen with a view toward developing an approach that allows for a clearer understanding of the adjustment process. In reality, of course, reported EPS would be adjusted upward or downward for various reconciling items. An example of an upward adjustment would be the adding back to EPS of the effect of an unjustified accounting cushion arising from overestimated warranty provisions or bad debt provisions.)

Reported EPS	$10.00
Deductions from reported EPS in order to arrive at an "acceptable quality" EPS	
Unjustified cutbacks in discretionary costs (e.g., advertising) as a percent of sales	.02
A decline in the ratio of bad debts to sales that is not warranted by experience	.03
One-time gains (gain on the sale of land) that are not expected to recur over the long run	.04
Income derived from the sale of acquired assets that were recorded at suppressed amounts at the time of a pooling transaction	.05
Inventory profits	.06
Accounting changes designed to bolster earnings (LIFO to FIFO)	.07
Lower pension expense arising from an unrealistic change in pension assumptions (increase in the actuarially assumed interest rate)	.08
Increase in deferred expenditures that do not have future economic benefit	.09
Items included in inventory which were previously expensed (labor, interest, administrative costs), assuming such items have no future utility	.02
Items included in plant and equipment that were previously expensed (e.g., maintenance costs)	.03
Lower provision (relative to prior years) for cost overruns on long-term construction contracts	.04
Increase in expenses (relative to prior years) charged to reserve accounts	.05
Unjustified reduction in reserve accounts	.06
Incremental capitalized interest relative to prior year	.07
Amount of underaccrual of expenses (or reserve provision)	.08
One-time earnings increment arising from a change in revenue recognition policy	.09
Lower effective tax rate arising from a one-time tax benefit, such as a foreign tax credit, that now becomes prohibited	.02
"Acceptable Quality" EPS	$9.10

REPAIR

- Incur expenditures needed for future successful operations.
- Make realistic expense and liability provisions.
- Provide for realistic recognition of revenue.

- Avoid cutting costs necessary for successful operations.
- Write-down overstated assets.

PREVENTION TECHNIQUES
- Use realistic accounting methods and assumptions.
- Avoid manipulative accounting practices.
- Avoid deferring expenditures with questionable future benefits.
- Diversify operations.
- Enter countercyclical lines of business.
- Reduce risk exposure.
- Combat the adverse effects of inflation on the business.
- Adjust the cost structure more toward variable costs than toward fixed costs.

SPILLOVER EFFECTS.   Poor earnings quality:
- Increases the cost of borrowing
- Increases debt relative to equity financing because investors are less inclined to buy the company's stock because of its perceived lower quality
- May lead to business failure because of the risk assigned to the company on account of its dubious earnings quality
- Decreases the market price of stock and bonds
- Lowers the credit rating
- Increases employee turnover because of the higher probability of business failure
- Increases the collateral requirements for loans

Problem: Unstable Operations and Earnings

IDENTIFYING SYMPTOMS.   Fluctuating sales, costs, and profitability over time.

CAUSES.   If operations are subject to risk from industrial, corporate, political, or economic factors, there will be uncertainty. If there is a high turnover rate in management, operating policy will be inconsistent.

If a change in outside auditors is made, the financial reporting system may be affected because of different audit approaches and philosophies. If accounting changes are made in methods and estimates, accounting policies will be inconsistent.

Variability in operations may also exist because

- Management is taking excessive risks.

- A high degree of financial leverage is preventing the firm from meeting principal and interest on debt when earnings decline. (A high degree of operating leverage means a cost structure containing significant fixed costs. As volume decreases, fixed costs cannot be cut in the short run, resulting in a dramatic falloff in profits.)

- The company is too susceptible to the business cycle and seasonality.

- When the source and cost of raw materials for production are unreliable, instability in manufacturing operations and earnings fluctuation result.

- Product sales derived from a few large industrial users are risky.

- The business is operating in an unstable political environment.

MEASUREMENT AND ANALYSIS.   We rely on the repetitiveness of occurrence in *projecting* future earnings. Therefore, we need to separate stable elements of income and expense from those that are random and erratic. Earnings derived from recurring transactions related to the basic business of the company is of *higher quality* than those resulting from isolated transactions.

Determine the extent to which earnings reflect one-time gains and losses that are *not* part of the basic business of the firm, because they distort the current year's income as a predictor of future earnings. For example, a one-time gain will result in a higher than normal level of earnings for the year. As a result, such items should be eliminated from net income in determining relevant earnings.

To determine the extent to which net income is affected by distortive elements, the percent of one-time gains and losses to net income and to sales should be computed.

Example: The following figures are extracted from company C's comparative income statements:

	19X0	19X1	19X2
Sales	$100,000	$105,000	$113,000
Net income	20,000	22,000	27,000
Net one-time gains (one-time gains less one-time losses)	5,000	7,000	10,000
The percent of net one-time gains to sales and to net income are:			
Net one-time gains to sales	5.0%	6.7%	8.8%
Net one-time gains to net income	25.0%	31.8%	37.0%

The rising percentage of net one-time gains to sales and to net income indicates a deterioration in earnings quality.

Determine the trends in operating income sources (sales) and non-operating income sources (lease income, royalty income) over the last five years. Nonoperating income may be more stable, and therefore of higher quality, than operating income. Evaluate nonoperating income to determine the extent to which it is recurring and acts as a cushion to the stability of total income.

Look at the current environment to see if any changes in demand for the company's products or services are anticipated. If you conclude that greater recurrence and dependability is indicated by one or more nonoperating income sources, look at the trend in the percentage of such nonoperating items to sales and to net income. Rising trends reflect higher earnings quality. In evaluating the nature and riskiness of a business, examine the stability of the earnings trend. Of course the trend in income is considerably more significant than its absolute size.

Earnings stability can be measured by average reported earnings, average pessimistic earnings, standard deviation, coefficient of variation, instability index, and beta. When using these techniques, the earnings trend should be looked at over a long period (ranging from five to ten years). The greater the variation in earnings for a business as indicated by these measures, the worse it is for the business.

1. *Average reported earnings.*   The average earnings (in five years) will smooth out abnormal and erratic income statement components as well as cyclical effects on the business. Thus, the average earnings figure results in a better measure of earning power than that of net income for a particular year.

2. *Average pessimistic earnings.*   This is the average earnings based on the *worst* possible business activity. Such minimum earnings are only useful in situations where the business is quite risky and you wish to provide for such risk. The first step is to restate the reported earnings to minimum earnings for each year. Then the minimum earnings for all years are totaled and finally divided by the number of years involved.

3. *Standard deviation*

$$\text{S.D.} = \sqrt{\frac{\Sigma(y - \bar{y})^2}{n}}$$

where y = reported earnings for period t
    $\bar{y}$ = average earnings
    n = number of years

A high standard deviation indicates greater risk, since it measures the variability of earnings around expected earnings. It is an absolute measure of instability.

4. *Coefficient of variation*

$$\text{C.V.} = \frac{\text{S.D.}}{\bar{y}}$$

The coefficient of variation represents the degree of risk per unit of return. It is used to appraise relative instability in earnings among companies. The higher the coefficient of variation in earnings of a business, the higher the risk in its earnings stream.

5. *Instability index of earnings*

$$I = \sqrt{\frac{\Sigma(y - y^T)^2}{n}}$$

Where y^T = trend earnings for period t, and is calculated by:

$$y^T = a + bt$$

where a = dollar intercept
    b = slope of trend line
    t = time period

A simple trend equation solved by computer is used to determine trend income. The index reflects the deviation between actual income and trend income. The higher the index, the lower the quality of earnings associated with the business.

6. *Beta.*   Beta is determined via a computer run by the following equation:

$$r_{jt} = \alpha_j + B_j r_{Mt} + E_{jt}$$

where r_{jt} = return on security j for period t
    α_j = constant
    B_j = beta for security j
    r_{Mt} = return on a market index such as the New York Stock
        Exchange Index
    E_{jt} = error term

Beta is a measure of undiversifiable risk of a stock. It helps analyze the risk-return trade-off. A high beta means that the company's stock price has shown more fluctuation than that of the change in the market index, indicating that it is a risky security. High variability in stock price may indicate greater business risk associated with the firm, instability in its past earnings trend, or lower earnings quality. For example, a beta of 1.6 means that the firm's stock price rises or falls 60 percent more than the market. Over time, a company's stock may have had a positive beta in some years and a negative beta in other years.

REPAIR

- Enter into a forward contract to take delivery of raw materials at the set price at a future date. The uncertainty of a raw material source may be corrected by vertical integration or entering into a joint venture. Establish alternative sources of supply for raw materials. Plan ahead by reviewing prices of raw materials and their current and future availability in trade and financial publications.

- Enter into foreign currency future contracts to lock in a fixed rate.

- Reduce instability in earnings due to a high fixed cost structure by moving toward a variable cost structure. Attempt to increase the ratio of variable costs to fixed costs.

- Protect and maintain a reliable source of earnings, such as service contracts or replacement parts on products previously sold.

- Provide for adequate legal liability insurance to guard against possible lawsuits.

- Develop or promote a product line of low-unit-cost items to provide income during a strong economy and serve as a cushion against declining demand during recession.

- Add products having different seasonal appeal and demand.

PREVENTION TECHNIQUES

- Undertake a risk-management program to find ways to curtail risk.

- Minimize uncertainty by entering countercyclical or noncyclical lines of business.

- Promote the production and sale of products that are less affected by the business cycle.

- Emphasize stable products and better-grade investments.

- Diversify the customer base to provide protection from adverse changes in the economy or in one or two industries.

SPILLOVER EFFECTS

- When operations and profits are unstable it is hard to predict future earnings and stock price.

- Variability in earnings and uncertainty in overall operations will result in a lower market price of stock, lower issuance price for bond offerings, higher cost of financing to compensate for the increased risk, and lower credit ratings.

- The potential impact of uncertainties facing a business may be of such magnitude that net income has little predictive value.

See also EXCESSIVE OPERATING LEVERAGE, LACK OF DIVERSIFICATION, POOR-QUALITY EARNINGS, and REVENUE BASE EROSION.

Problem: Unstable Income

IDENTIFYING SYMPTOMS

- The existence of an opportunist and temporary market (such as the early market for computers)
- Extra product demand, coupled with a sharp upward acceleration of prices
- Sudden and unexpected developments that depress revenue
- Variances in selling prices and costs.

CAUSES

- The product mix is *positively correlated,* meaning that demand for the products moves upward or downward together. (Examples of such products are automobiles, tires, and steel.)
- The company is unable to introduce new products.
- The product line consists primarily of items that are declining in demand and/or products in their initial stages of research and development.
- The product is nearing the end of its life cycle.
- The customer base consists of a few large concerns.
- The company's main income is based on a single significant contract (e.g., government contract) or a single product.
- The temporary income is a high percentage of total revenue.
- The company's products are susceptible to changes in the business cycle and seasonality.
- The product line lacks diversification.
- The product line is subject to rapid changes in demand and taste.
- Export sales to a major foreign market is subject to sudden disappearance when that country develops its own domestic production.

MEASUREMENT AND ANALYSIS. Determine the extent to which earnings reflect unstable sources of income that are not part of the basic business of the firm. Operating income (sales) should be of a higher quality than nonoperating income (e.g., interest revenue) because it represents the earnings generated from selling the company's products. However, nonoperating income may be more stable than sales, and if so, is of a higher quality than operating income. Evaluate nonoperating income to determine the extent to which it is recurring and acts as a cushion to the stability of total income.

Stability in product revenue can be determined by computing the standard deviation in sales over five to ten years. As mentioned in UNSTABLE OPERATIONS AND EARNINGS, standard deviation equals:

$$\text{Standard deviation} = \sqrt{\frac{\Sigma(y - \bar{y})^2}{n}}$$

where y = reported earnings for period t
y = average earnings
n = number of years

A high standard deviation indicates instability in income.

A coefficient of variation may also be computed to appraise relative instability with other competing companies.

$$\text{Coefficient of variation} = \frac{\text{S.D.}}{\bar{y}}$$

Example:

19X0	$100,000
19X1	110,000
19X2	80,000
19X3	120,000
19X4	140,000

The standard deviation in sales is:

$$\text{Standard deviation} = \sqrt{\frac{\Sigma(y - \bar{y})^2}{n}}$$

$$\bar{y} = \Sigma \frac{y}{n} = \frac{100,000 + 110,000 + 80,000 + 120,000 + 140,000}{5}$$

$$= \frac{550,000}{5} = 110,000$$

Year	$(y - \bar{y})$	$(y - \bar{y})^2$
19X0	−10,000	100,000,000
19X1	0	0
19X2	−30,000	900,000,000
19X3	+10,000	100,000,000
19X4	+30,000	900,000,000
Total		2,000,000,000

$$\text{Standard deviation} = \sqrt{\frac{2,000,000,000}{5}} = \sqrt{400,000,000} = 20,000$$

The coefficient of variation in sales is:

$$\text{Coefficient of variation} = \frac{\text{standard deviation}}{\bar{y}} \quad \frac{20,000}{110,000} = 18.2\%$$

The more the product line is susceptible to variances in volume, price, and cost, the greater the revenue instability. Chart the variability in quantity, selling price, and cost of each major product line over one or more periods of time.

Evaluate how much revenue is derived from growth, mature, declining, and developmental products.

REPAIR

- Attempt to derive further revenues after the initial sales contact.

- First-time sales should be supported by maintenance contracts, follow-up sales (like those for batteries and flashcubes in the case of cameras), and replacement parts.

- Diversify the product line with *negatively correlated* (noncorrelated) items to provide overall stability in income. With negative correlation, revenue obtained from one product increases at the same time that revenue obtained from the other products decreases. (Examples of negatively correlated products are air conditioners and heaters.)

- Expand the product line to include additional complementary products. (For a firm selling air conditioners and heaters, complementary products could include insulating materials, thermostats, and home improvement materials.)

PREVENTIVE TECHNIQUES

- Emphasize products that are least affected by the business cycle.

- Attempt to change product lines to more stable products.

- Develop a piggyback product base (similar products associated with the basic business).

- Sell low-priced products as well as more expensive goods as a built-in hedge in inflationary and recessionary periods.

- Move toward necessity items, which perform well in both good and bad economic times.

- Avoid novelty and nonessential goods.

- Sell to diversified industries to protect against cyclical turns in the economy.

- Reduce exposure to the effects of the economic cycle by entering noncyclical or countercyclical lines of business.

- Diversify geographically to reduce susceptibility to economic downturns.

SPILLOVER EFFECTS.   Revenue instability leads to vacillating and erratic earnings and will negatively affect the market price of the company's debt and equity securities. The uncertainty of the income stream will make the firm's future more risky.

See also WEAK SALES MIX.

Problem: Low Price/Earnings Ratio

IDENTIFYING SYMPTOM.   Low market price of company stock.

CAUSES

- Investors lack confidence in the company's financial stability or growth potential. This weakness may be due to the company's financial position, its trend in earnings, or the investing public's perception of the quality of its earnings.

- The market price of a company's stock does not increase proportionally with its earnings per share.

- Investors who believe that the company will be less profitable in the future value the stock lower than its current earnings would seem to indicate.

MEASUREMENT AND ANALYSIS

$$\text{Price/earnings ratio} = \frac{\text{market price per share}}{\text{earnings per share}}$$

The company's price/earnings (P/E) ratio should be compared to the price/earnings ratios of competing companies in the same industry, and with those of other companies. P/E ratios may be found in financial service publications. Reference should also be made to the price/earnings ratios of the market.

Example: The market prices per share of stock are $20 and $24, respectively, for 19X8 and 19X9. The earnings per share for those years are $2 and $3, respectively. The price/earnings ratios are computed as:

		19X8	19X9
P/E ratio =	$\dfrac{\text{market price per share}}{\text{earnings per share}}$	$\dfrac{\$20}{\$2} = 10$	$\dfrac{\$24}{\$3} = 8$

REPAIR.   Convince prospective investors that the company's low-price earnings multiple means that its stock is undervalued and is a bargain.

PREVENTION TECHNIQUES

- Improve the company's overall financial condition, including balance sheet posture and earnings.

- Reduce risk.
- Enhance operational stability.
- Expand, diversify, and sell off unprofitable branches and divisions.
- Hire more successful managers.
- Develop a promotional campaign to emphasize the firm's history, the quality of its products, and its potential for economic growth.

SPILLOVER EFFECTS.   A low price-earnings ratio means that the company may be a poor investment. As a result, investors are likely to stay away, thereby further depressing the market price of the company's stock. The failure to attract equity investors may cause the creditors to demand a rise in the interest rate. The higher cost of financing will reduce earnings.

6

Costs Cut into Profits

Excessive costs must be controlled. They will eat into profits and may possibly result in losses. Cost reduction and control programs should be implemented to eliminate excess fat and inefficiency in the organization. However, costs needed for future viability, such as those for repairs, research and development, and advertising, should not be reduced. Management may have a problem formulating financial decisions because cost information is inadequate or distorted. If raw materials are unavailable or are only available at exorbitant rates, manufacturing problems will result. The company may be unable to introduce new products or services for future growth because of high up-front costs. Incorrect pricing based on high or erroneous cost figures will lead to declining earnings.

Problem: Excessive Labor Costs

IDENTIFYING SYMPTOMS

- Inadequate funding for pension and health care benefits
- A decline in earnings because wage and fringe benefit costs are not controlled
- Excessive workmen's compensation claims
- A high degree of employee turnover
- Theft and sabotage of company assets

CAUSES

- "Giving in" to unions
- Poor employee performance and productivity
- Lack of supervision
- Inadequate training
- Obsolete machinery and equipment
- Inefficient production scheduling
- Alcohol and drug abuse

- Hiring the wrong employees or hiring more employees than necessary
- Absenteeism

MEASUREMENT AND ANALYSIS

- Compute the trend in the ratio of labor costs to total costs, labor costs to sales, and labor costs to net income.
- Examine postretirement payouts to retirees.
- Compare the company's employee benefits with those provided by other companies in the industry.
- Compute the rate and efficiency variances for direct and indirect labor costs. (*See* ACTUAL COSTS EXCEED STANDARD COSTS in Chapter 9.)

REPAIR

- Negotiate with unions for give-backs in wages, fringe benefits, hours, and other working conditions.
- Pay the minimum wage possible for a particular position, give minimal wage increases, or if possible freeze salaries.
- Lay off employees to cut payroll.
- Institute a furlough (delay) in pay, or reduce working hours and workdays.
- Improve supervision by factory foremen and other managers.
- Do not have more employees assigned to a specific task than are needed.
- Use temporary and per-diem personnel.
- Prepare employee time sheets, so time is monitored and charged to specific jobs and customers.
- Control health care costs by:

  Increasing deductibles and reducing reimbursement payments to lower premium rates
  Placing "caps" on certain benefits
  Requiring employees to contribute to their health plan
  Switching to cheaper carriers
  Instituting low-cost health care centers (e.g., HIP, HMO)
  Requiring second opinions before operations
  Removing selected health care coverage from the package
  Eliminating retiree health care benefits
  Terminating coverage for beneficiaries
  Encouraging preventive health care

- Institute a stock-based compensation plan.
- Give inefficient workers the option of transferring to a new facility or position.
- Provide terminated employees with assistance in locating new employment.
- Operate with small, central staffs.
- Increase selling prices for goods and service.

PREVENTION TECHNIQUES

- Hire a competent union negotiator or labor attorney and support binding arbitration.
- Tie any increased wages to improvements in productivity.
- Design and implement actions to resolve such employee problems as low productivity or poor workmanship.
- Improve production scheduling.
- Reassign workers to improve efficiency.
- Find out the reasons for absenteeism and low productivity.
- Offer early retirement incentives.
- Prepare a newsletter to communicate to employees about the company's financial problems, how employees can help, and the possible adverse effects on the employees if conditions do not improve.
- Conduct periodic meetings with this stated policy in mind.
- Keep equipment in proper working order.
- Introduce continuous safety checks.
- Develop proper job descriptions.
- Evaluate the personnel department to make sure it is hiring the right people.
- Integrate the personnel staff into the planning process to enable them to evaluate job descriptions so that only the best-qualified employees are hired.
- Downsize the number of employees if future business is uncertain.
- Evaluate senior executive compensation, staffing, and performance.
- Reduce executive perks, including bonuses and expense accounts.
- Offer cash bonuses to employees who contribute workable ideas to save costs.

SPILLOVER EFFECTS. The failure to cap employee salaries and fringe benefits will drain cash and earnings and can lead to serious financial problems. Friction resulting from management-worker disputes may result in strikes and physical damage to property, plant, and equipment.

See also INADEQUATE COST CONTROLS and UNFUNDED RETIREMENT BENEFITS.

Problem: Excessive Operating Leverage

IDENTIFYING SYMPTOMS

- Significant earnings instability, resulting from small changes in sales
- A high break-even point, indicating that more sales dollars are needed to cover total costs in order to earn a zero profit
- Difficulty adjusting costs to meet a changing revenue base

CAUSE. Significant fixed costs are usually to blame. If sales decline, profitability will sharply fall off because fixed costs are constant. The business usually can only cut fixed costs in the long term.

MEASUREMENT AND ANALYSIS. Operating leverage can be measured using the following ratios:

1. Fixed costs to total costs
2. Percentage change in operating income to the percentage change in sales volume
3. Net income to fixed charges

An increase in the first two or a decrease in the third may indicate higher fixed charges, possibly resulting in greater instability in operations and earnings.

When high operating leverage is combined with highly elastic product demand, earnings will fluctuate sharply. Such conditions, though undesirable and leading to lower earnings quality, may be inherent in an entity's operations (i.e., in the airline and auto industries).

The effects of operating leverage diminish as revenue increases above the break-even point because the bases to which increases in earnings are compared get progressively larger. It may thus be advantageous to analyze the relationship between sales and the break-even point when evaluating a company's earnings stability. A company with a high break-even point is quite vulnerable to economic declines.

REPAIR

- To the extent possible, slash fixed costs.
- Expand sales to cover remaining ones.

PREVENTION TECHNIQUE.   Move toward a cost structure of variable costs rather than fixed costs. The object is to increase the percentage of variable costs to total costs. Variable costs can be adjusted more easily than fixed costs to meet a decline in product demand.

SPILLOVER EFFECTS.   An excessive degree of operating leverage will sharply reduce profitability if sales decline, particularly in a recession. Failure to cut fixed costs in the long term may ultimately force the company into bankruptcy, as its cash is drained to meet these static and recurring charges.

See also PRODUCT OR SERVICE DOES NOT BREAK EVEN.

Problem: Inadequate Cost Controls

IDENTIFYING SYMPTOMS

- Large variances in the cash disbursement reports between various prices paid for identical quantities of the same raw materials
- Labor variances showing up on job cost sheets due to:

  Differences in time spent performing identical tasks
  Different hourly rates for employee overtime needed to solve unforeseen scheduling problems

- Excessive raw materials required to manufacture a product

CAUSES

- Lax or ineffective purchasing procedures
- Lack of management control, resulting in inefficient operations and products of minimal or unacceptable quality

MEASUREMENT AND ANALYSIS

- Instruct each department to set up standards for each product line.
- Plot the data corresponding to each standard. Visualization of the data creates an extended visibility of how the product is performing. Correlation of the standards to potential problems helps correct the situation before the difficulties reach crises levels.
- Measure the variance in costs—the difference between the actual costs and the standard costs—inherent in the operations of the

organization. (*Standard costs* are preestablished costs that serve as targets against which the *actual costs* of production can be measured.) Then use this analysis to determine the profitability and efficiency of operations.

See ACTUAL COSTS EXCEED BUDGETED COSTS and ACTUAL COSTS EXCEED STANDARD COSTS in Chapter 9 for the computation and analysis of variances.

REPAIR

- Enforce a strict cost control and containment program. Hold each purchasing agent responsible for controlling material costs and each production supervisor liable for maintaining standard labor costs.

- Arbitrate a price increase on a contracted project that is losing money. Perhaps the project was contracted out as a fixed-priced program.

- Reduce the fluctuations of yields for raw materials purchased. Decrease the spending for raw materials by increasing the yields of the product. This may be accomplished by frequent inspections during the product manufacturing phase. (*Yield* refers to the quantity of finished output produced from a predetermined or standard combination and amount of inputs, such as direct material or direct labor.)

- Tighten the controls on spending, both for raw materials and for production facilities and equipment.

PREVENTION TECHNIQUES

- Use Statistical Quality Control (SQC) techniques to ensure that the costs are within a normal (tolerable) range.

- Use Economic Order Quantity (EOQ) and Material Requirement Planning (MRP) analysis for raw material ordering. (*See* DEFICIENT INVENTORY BALANCES and EXCESSIVE ORDERING AND CARRYING COSTS in Chapter 3.) Develop agreements with raw material suppliers for set prices and reliable delivery schedules. Avoid multiple small orders where freight charges can cause costs to rise sharply.

- Create a more flexible cost budget. Cost planning allows the cost center to regulate the way it spends money. Set early warning limits on expenditures to trigger a "red flag" before the cost goes out of control. Educate the employees on the effects of inadequate cost control.

- Delegate certain employees to be "watchdogs" for the yields and raw material usage. Teach them Statistical Process Control (SPC) to help control and expedite the process for a product. SPC is a technique that helps estimate the probability that a production process is in control. This should help improve the yields and maintain a consistent quality for a product.

SPILLOVER EFFECTS.   If the costs cannot be controlled, it may be necessary to reduce staff and other operating expenditures to maintain profitability. Recapitalization may not be possible if there is a loss of money due to poor cost control. If the cost control problem continues, diminished profitability, insolvency, and bankruptcy may be inevitable.

See also LACK OF COST INFORMATION, DISTORTED COST INFORMATION, EXCESSIVE LABOR COSTS, LOW RATE OF RETURN, and UNPROFITABLE PROFIT CENTERS.

Problem: Lack of Cost Information

IDENTIFYING SYMPTOMS

- The accounting system provides incomplete or inaccurate cost data.
- Wrong financial decisions are being made based on unsupported or deficient supporting data.

CAUSES

- Incompetent or inexperienced staff
- Budget restrictions, resulting in a cutback in recording important costs, production management, and financial reports
- Costs improperly classified in the records
- Costs not broken down into variable and fixed costs, preventing break-even and cost-volume-profit analysis
- Failure to prepare detailed or adequate cost budgets
- Use of an outdated cost accounting system that misstates the costs of products or services

MEASUREMENT AND ANALYSIS

- Examine the trend in costs over time.
- Set standards for costs.
- Compare budgeted costs to actual costs and investigate any deviation.
- Track fluctuation in costs.
- Examine the interrelationship among costs.

REPAIR

- Take inflation into account when estimating and analyzing costs.
- Hire competent cost accountants.
- Insist that personnel take courses in cost accounting.
- Modernize the cost accounting system, using such systems as Just-In-Time costing (JIT) and Activity-Based Costing (ABC). (ABC is a system that focuses on activities as the fundamental cost objects.)
- Allocate costs to appropriate divisions and departments.

PREVENTION TECHNIQUES

- Hire an experienced cost accounting consultant to identify weaknesses in the cost accounting system and recommend areas for improvement.
- Computerize the cost accounting system to incorporate the latest technological developments.
- Use up-to-date quantitative techniques to track costs.
- Have departmental managers identify cost information they feel they need but are not getting. Managers should participate in the budgeting and cost accounting process because they have an intimate knowledge of matters affecting their particular operations.
- Have costs managed by responsibility centers at the lowest practical level.
- Base transfer prices for internal transfers within the company for assembled products or services on a negotiated market value.
- Conduct a continual internal audit of the cost accounting system to identify and correct weaknesses as they arise.

SPILLOVER EFFECTS.   If cost information is inadequate, the business may not be able to control its costs, since it may not know the actual costs incurred by each responsibility center or segment. Cost overruns may decrease company profitability. By understating expenses, the company may be selling products for less than it costs to produce them. Bid prices on contracts may also be understated, resulting in operating losses. If management is not aware of actual operating costs incurred, it cannot plan adequately.

See also DISTORTED COST INFORMATION.

Problem: Distorted Cost Information

IDENTIFYING SYMPTOMS

- Loss of competitiveness in the marketplace
- Loss of contract bids due to inaccurate product pricing
- Loss of contribution due to poor product mix
- Hard-to-explain outcomes of bids and profit margins
- Surprisingly high profits on products or services that are difficult to produce
- A desire by managers to drop products or services that appear profitable
- No complaints from customers about price increases
- Misleadingly high or low product prices

CAUSES

- Wrong calculations for variable and fixed costs
- One product carrying more of the fixed cost than the others

MEASUREMENT AND ANALYSIS. Many companies use a traditional cost system, such as job-order costing or process costing, or some hybrid of the two. This traditional system may distort product cost information. In fact, companies selling multiple products are making critical decisions about product pricing, making bids, or product mix based on inaccurate cost data. Usually the problem is not with assigning the costs of direct labor or direct materials. These prime costs are traceable to individual products, and most conventional cost systems are designed to ensure that this tracing takes place. However, the assignment of overhead costs to individual products is another matter. Using the traditional methods of assigning overhead costs to products, using a single predetermined overhead rate based on any single activity measure, can produce distorted product costs.

REPAIR. Use Activity-Based Costing (ABC) with multiple cost drivers. (A *cost driver* provides the basis for allocating a cost to a department.) Cost drivers that indirectly measure the consumption of an activity usually measure the number of transactions associated with that activity. It is possible to replace a cost driver that directly measures consumption with one that only indirectly measures it without loss of accuracy, provided that the quantities of activity consumed per transaction are stable for each product. In such a case, the indirect cost driver has a high correlation and can be used. Examples of cost drivers include direct labor hours, square footage, and number of orders placed.

PREVENTION TECHNIQUES. The financial manager needs to carefully evaluate cost-driver considerations in designing a product costing system. A costing system using multiple cost drivers is more costly to implement and use, but it may save millions.

- Use Activity-Based Costing (ABC) to provide more accurate information about product costs. It can help managers make better decisions about product design, pricing, marketing, and mix, and encourages continual operating improvements.

- Use a Just-In-Time (JIT) costing system to convert indirect costs to direct costs. This conversion reduces the need to use multiple cost drivers to assign overhead costs to products, thus enhancing product-costing accuracy. For example, under the JIT system, workers on the production line will do plant maintenance and setups, while under traditional systems these activities were done by other workers classified as indirect labor. JIT, coupled with ABC, can greatly improve product costing accuracy.

- Confirm total fixed costs and assign the proper fixed cost per unit to the product before releasing it to the market.

- Produce prototype products to determine the expected yield to establish the cost of the product.

SPILLOVER EFFECTS. Inaccuracies in calculating the overhead cost per unit can lead to poor decisions about pricing, product mix, or contract bidding.

If the cost distortion is high, the product may be overpriced. High-priced products may be less price competitive and have lower sales than expected. If the cost distortion is too high, the product may be considered too expensive to produce.

If the cost distortion is too low, the product can lose profits for the company and even fail to achieve the break-even point. Losses or loss products may force the company to reduce staff or facility size. In either case, lost business can hurt the company's future.

See also LACK OF COST INFORMATION.

Problem: Supplies Increase in Cost or Are Unavailable

IDENTIFYING SYMPTOMS

- Manufacturing delays
- Low stocking of supplies and raw materials
- Supplier strikes
- Actual costs exceeding budgeted costs

- Cash flow deficiencies
- Failure to meet customer orders

CAUSES

- Strikes at suppliers
- Political unrest
- Inflation or economic uncertainty
- Poor materials planning
- Inaccurate forecasts and budgets

MEASUREMENT AND ANALYSIS

- Determine whether the business is highly dependent on unreliable sources of supply.
- Examine delivery problems from suppliers in the past.
- Evaluate the trend in raw material costs to sales over ten years.
- Appraise the trend in the company's production activity over time, and identify the reasons.

REPAIR

- Increase selling prices.
- Seek alternative sources of supplies.
- Substitute cheaper raw materials.
- Improve production efficiency.
- Initiate legal action if a contractual agreement has been violated.

PREVENTION TECHNIQUES

- Stock up on raw materials.
- Enter into futures contracts for delivery at a later date at a set price.
- Self-manufacture the items in question.
- Enter into long-term supply arrangements.
- Acquire the supplier.
- Review trade publications for potential problems.
- Use vertical integration to reduce the price and supply risks of raw materials.

SPILLOVER EFFECTS

- Profitability will decrease unless selling prices are also increased.
- Cash flow will diminish because of higher costs.
- Production cutbacks will be necessary, resulting in less sales volume for your product.
- Dissatisfied customers may shift to competitors.
- There will be higher risk and uncertainty regarding future earnings.

See also EXCESSIVE COST-TO-PRODUCTION VOLUME.

Problem: Cost Reductions Hamper Development

IDENTIFYING SYMPTOMS

- Declining sales
- Loss of customers
- Diminishing profitability
- Layoffs and reduction of costs needed for future survival

CAUSES

- Lack of available cost information
- Postponement of necessary major repairs and upkeep
- Failure to take into account the benefits of projected expenditure
- Poor economy and/or business conditions
- Deficient financial planning
- Failure to properly use cost analysis
- Nonproductive assets and personnel

MEASUREMENT AND ANALYSIS.   The trend in the ratio of cost cuts to total costs will reveal the extent of the austerity program. A comparison should also be made between costs and sales over several periods. The revenue lost because of cost reduction programs should be noted (the market share lost, for example, because of failure to advertise).

REPAIR

- Better cost analysis to determine the benefit derived from incurring cost.
- Cost management to assure that costs are at the minimal operating level without adversely affecting business.

PREVENTION TECHNIQUES

- Determine exactly where costs cuts can be made with minimal adverse financial consequences.
- Hire an independent consultant.
- Make more use of budgets and financial models.

SPILLOVER EFFECTS

- A long-term decline in profitability
- A lower growth rate
- Failure to maintain a competitive position because of an inability to promote new product or service innovations
- Erosion of the customer base
- Failure to maintain up-to-date accounting records

See also EXCESSIVE LABOR COSTS and REDUCED DISCRETIONARY COSTS HURT THE BUSINESS.

Problem: Reduced Discretionary Costs Hurt the Business

IDENTIFYING SYMPTOMS.   A reduction in advertising, repairs and maintenance, research and development, training, and so on.

CAUSE.   The business is starved of needed expenses.

MEASUREMENT AND ANALYSIS.   Analysts should determine:

1. The trend in discretionary costs as a percentage of net sales.
2. The trend in discretionary costs to the assets with which they are associated.

Declining trends may indicate a future deterioration in operations. For example, a declining trend in repairs and maintenance as a percentage of fixed assets may indicate a company's failure to maintain capital facilities.

Index numbers may be used to compare current discretionary expenditures with base-year expenditures. An *index number* is simply a ratio of a current-year amount to a base-year (most typical year) amount.

Analysts should note whether the current level of discretionary costs is consistent with the company's previous trends and with its present and future requirements.

REPAIR. Reinstate realistic discretionary costs.

PREVENTION TECHNIQUE. Before cost cutting, analyze the long-term financial and operational effects of doing so on the business.

SPILLOVER EFFECTS

- Failure to keep abreast of current developments
- Break-down of machinery, leading to production curtailments
- Improperly trained staff
- Decreased market share
- Failure to develop new products
- Deterioration in employee morale
- Loss to competition
- Long-term decline in corporate profitability and earning power

See also COST REDUCTIONS HAMPER DEVELOPMENT.

Problem: Up-Front Costs Impede Project Authorization

IDENTIFYING SYMPTOMS

- Significant outlay of expenditures
- High percentage of project rejection due to high start-up costs

CAUSES

- Inadequate financial planning
- Deficient financial position, including low liquidity, failure to obtain financing, and deficient budgeting proposals

MEASUREMENT AND ANALYSIS

- Examine the ratio of up-front costs to total costs of a proposed project.
- Compare budgeted costs to actual costs.
- Compare the number of project rejections due to high initial costs to total projects available.

REPAIR

- Obtain adequate funding for projects from both debt and/or equity sources.
- Set up a joint venture with another business.
- Get venture capital financing by selling equity interest.
- Sell assets to raise cash.

PREVENTION TECHNIQUES

- Better planning at the proposal stage
- Establishing open lines of credit
- Postponing expenditures where feasible
- Dividing large projects into smaller, self-contained units
- Joining with other companies that have a successful record of product and service innovation

SPILLOVER EFFECTS

- Lower earning potential and growth
- Inability to issue additional shares of stock because prospective investors view the business as a poor risk due to lack of growth potential
- A competitive disadvantage because of lack of innovative projects

Problem: Pricing Lowers Profits

IDENTIFYING SYMPTOM.   Sales lead to lower profits even though cost is minimized and the optimal quantity is produced and sold.

CAUSE.   An upward price adjustment cannot offset the cost of selling to slow-paying customers.

MEASUREMENT AND ANALYSIS. Calculate the price elasticity of demand of the product or service. Price elasticity, denoted with ep, is the ratio of a percentage change in quantity demanded (Q) to a percentage change in price (p).

$$ep = \frac{dQ/Q}{dp/p} = \frac{dQ}{dp} \times \frac{p}{Q}$$

where dQ/dp is simply the slope of the demand function $Q = (p)$. We classify the price elasticity demand in three categories:

If ep > 1, elastic

ep = 1, unitary

ep < 1, inelastic

Example: The demand function is given as $Q = 200 - 6p$. The price elasticity at $p = 4$ is computed as follows:

First,

$$Q = 200 - 6(4) = 176$$

Since $dQ/dp = -6$, the ep at $p = 4$ is:

$$ep = -6 \times \left(\frac{4}{176} \right) = -0.136$$

This means that a 1 percent change in price will bring about a 0.14 percent change in demand. The product under study is considered price inelastic, since the ep is less than 1 in absolute value.

Economists have established the following relationships between price elasticity (ep) and total revenue (TR), which can aid a firm in setting its price.

Price	ep > 1	ep = 1	ep < 1
Price rises	TR falls	No change	TR rises
Price falls	TR rises	No change	TR falls

Firms must be aware of the elasticity of their own demand curves when they set product prices.

A profit-maximizing firm would never choose to lower its price in the inelastic range of its demand curve. Such a price decrease would only decrease total revenue and at the same time increase costs, since output would be rising. The result would be a drastic decrease in profits. In fact, when costs are rising and the product is inelastic, the firm would have no difficulty passing on the increases by raising the price to the customer.

On the other hand, when there are many substitutes and demand is quite elastic, increasing prices may lead to a reduction in total revenue rather than to an increase. The result may be lower profits rather than higher profits.

While the goal of virtually all companies is to increase their market share, the marketing strategy required to achieve profit maximization is to determine the optimal price. Companies need to focus on being profitable rather than on increasing the sales dollars. Firms must examine whether their pricing strategies are being used properly. Some of the most important pricing strategies include:

1. Premium pricing, which should result in a higher percentage return than the return on the standard model

2. Marginal pricing, which is appropriate when a company has an advantage over its competitors

A pricing strategy which maximizes profits must be developed before a product is introduced, and the price must be adjusted according to demand.

REPAIR.   Base pricing on market demand. Do test market analysis.

PREVENTION TECHNIQUES.   Pricing decisions must be made in recognition of their short-term and long-term effects on the enterprise. Accept short-term orders for less than factory costs if excess capacity exists and if the selling price quoted would cover the variable costs (i.e., a positive contribution margin).

SPILLOVER EFFECTS

- Poor pricing policies will lower profits.
- Acceptance of low-price special orders on too large a scale may drive down the market price.
- Decreases in average unit price will distort the figures used in break-even analyses, requiring these to be recalculated.
- An earnings-per-share decrease will result in a decrease in the value of the company.
- A company that fails to operate at an acceptable profit level will face possible insolvency and bankruptcy.

See also HIGHER PRICES REDUCE SALES and LOWERED PRICES SHRINK MARGINS.

7

Financing Undermines Business Development

A company may experience significant financial problems, adversely affecting the market price of its stocks and bonds. Its credit and bond ratings may deteriorate. It may be unable to obtain financing at reasonable rates and terms. The inability to issue new securities and negotiate loans will starve the business of funds it needs to operate. If loan provisions are violated, bankers could force the business into liquidation. If dividends are restricted because of a lack of cash, stockholders may decide to replace corporate management.

Problem: Market Price of Stock Falls

IDENTIFYING SYMPTOMS

- Less demand for the company's shares by investors.
- Brokerage research houses recommend that investors sell or avoid buying the company's stock.
- The company gets poor reviews in financial newspapers and magazines.
- The company becomes the target of a takeover attempt.
- The market value of the company's common stock is below its book value.
- Lenders place stringent credit requirements on the company.
- Financing costs are increasing.
- Previous sources of financing are no longer available.

CAUSES

- Market conditions
- Excessive business risk

- Quality of management
- Continuous operating losses
- Inconsistent earnings performance
- Foreseeable negative future economic developments in the company's line of business
- Foreign competition
- Government action
- Loss of key managerial personnel
- Cash flow problems
- A deficient financial position overall
- Poor return on stockholders' equity
- Not earning an expected profit
- Not keeping up-to-date technologically or with market conditions

MEASUREMENT AND ANALYSIS

- Determine the percentage drop in the market price of stock over time.
- Chart price changes to see their overall direction and movement.
- Identify times during the year when stock price is vulnerable.
- Compare the change in the market price of the company's stock to that of competing companies in the industry, to industry price changes, and to changes in major stock indexes.
- Chart P-E ratio (market price of stock divided by earnings per share) over time and compare it with the industry group's P-E ratio.

REPAIR

- Have company buy back its own shares.
- Improve earnings and overall financial position.
- Diversify to reduce risk.
- Issue preferred stock and bonds so as not to dilute further the market price of common stock.
- Issue securities privately rather than publicly.
- Have the board of directors issue a reverse stock split to increase market price per share.
- Establish dividend reinvestment programs, employee stock option plans, and issue stock rights to existing stockholders.

PREVENTION TECHNIQUES

- Meet with security analysts to explain the positive financial aspects of the company.
- Give interviews to reporters for financial newspapers so that they understand the favorable conditions of the company.
- Deny false rumors in the marketplace promptly.
- Hire an investment banker for advice about improving the market price of the shares.

SPILLOVER EFFECTS

- Management may be voted out of office.
- The sale of additional shares of the company's stock may be accelerated, thereby causing a further drop in the market price.
- The cost of financing may increase because of the company's perceived deteriorating financial position and difficulties.
- Sources of funds may be less available.
- The company may have to reorganize or be liquidated.
- Stock options held by executives and employees may be worth less.
- The company may appear to be a poor investment for the average or unsophisticated investor.

See also BANKRUPTCY LOOMS, BOND RATING DROPS, INADEQUATE LIQUIDITY, INSOLVENCY, UNSTABLE OPERATIONS AND EARNINGS, LOW PRICE/EARNINGS RATIO, POOR CREDIT RATING, and POOR PROFITABILITY AND GROWTH.

Problem: Bond Rating Drops

IDENTIFYING SYMPTOMS

- Company fails to make interest payments or to pay creditors and suppliers.
- Financial advisory services place the company on their "credit-watch lists."
- Credit reporting services downgrade the company's bond rating.

CAUSES

- Inability to make interest payments
- Lack of consistent performance

- Lower debt/equity ratio
- Declining working capital and cash flow position
- Poor balance-sheet posture

MEASUREMENT AND ANALYSIS

- Evaluate the financial statement information and the overall performance of the enterprise.
- Conduct horizontal, vertical, and ratio analysis.
- Calculate trend percentages, which is a form of horizontal analysis.
- Study the reports of business publications to determine how they feel about the company as an investment vehicle.
- Consult brokerage research reports.
- Compare the company's operating figures with industry norms and competitors.
- Study the company's cash flow statement.
- Calculate the liquidity and profitability ratios reflecting the company's ability to pay current liabilities and long-term debt.

REPAIR

- Ask the bond credit rating services what financial procedures they would prefer to see your company initiate to reverse the downgrade.
- If possible, institute their recommendations and inform both the bond rating services and the investing public of your undertaking and intention to improve the company's overall operating performance.
- If the current market interest rate has dropped, redeem existing bonds and issue new debt at the prevailing, lower market rate.
- Issue bonds that have a conversion feature that enables the bond holders to convert the bonds into either preferred or common stock at a time when the creditors consider it profitable to do so.
- Renegotiate a lower interest rate with lenders.
- Issue stock at a favorable price to provide equity funds so as to improve the mix in the capital structure by lowering the debt/equity ratio.
- Sell assets to pay debt.
- Use tangible assets as collateral for the sale of bonds.
- Establish a maximum debt ceiling that cannot be exceeded.

PREVENTION TECHNIQUES

- Reduce costs.
- Sell off assets.
- Diversify to reduce risk.
- Lengthen the maturity dates of bonds.
- Keep credit reporting agencies informed of the company's financial situation and plans.
- Defer the payment of loans for one year.
- Offer creditors the opportunity to convert their credit holdings into stock at a favorable conversion rate.
- Try to anticipate future conditions in the economy and money market.
- Do not overextend the company, either financially or operationally.
- Use the hedging approach to financing by matching the maturity dates of debt to the collection date or maturity date of assets.

SPILLOVER EFFECTS.   A downward bond rating will make it more difficult to borrow, which will result in increased interest costs. These increased costs will negatively affect earnings and cash flow.

See also EXCESSIVE DEBT, MARKET PRICE OF STOCK FALLS, and POOR CREDIT RATING.

Problem: Inability to Obtain Financing

IDENTIFYING SYMPTOMS

- Refusal of loan applications
- A limited line of credit
- Inability to attract bondholders and stockholders
- Financing at excessive or exorbitant interest rates
- Significant loan restrictions
- Pledging of company assets in return for loans

CAUSES

- Inadequate liquid reserves
- An increasing risk of insolvency

- Obsolete assets
- Poor earnings
- Excessive business risks
- Weak economic conditions

MEASUREMENT AND ANALYSIS. The failure to obtain financing may be evaluated by examining:

- The trend in financing obtained by source
- The ratio of loan applications denied to total loan applications
- The trend in the effective interest rate to borrow (interest divided by loan proceeds)
- The decline in the market price of a company's bonds and stocks
- A drop in bond ratings
- The trend showing the increased collateralization of assets

A higher ratio of sales to accounts payable indicates the company's inability to obtain short-term credit in the form of cost-free funds to finance sales growth.

REPAIR. To obtain financing the company must:

- Provide sufficient collateral
- Sell an equity interest in the business
- Agree to higher interest rates and loan restrictions
- Factor or assign receivables
- Sell or shut down unprofitable divisions or subsidiaries

PREVENTION TECHNIQUES

- Obtain open lines of credit with banks.
- Repay all loans promptly.
- Improve the company's overall financial position through cost cutting and layoffs.
- Cease production of unprofitable products or services.
- Lease assets instead of purchasing them.
- Extend and stagger payment dates of liabilities.
- Avoid excessive debt.
- Note those loan restrictions that the company may violate.

- Compare the current status of all loans to all loan compliance requirements to determine to what extent a safety buffer exists.
- Try to anticipate future conditions in the economy and money market.

SPILLOVER EFFECTS

- A deteriorating cash position
- Increased cost of capital
- Higher compensating balances
- Increased business risk
- Financial instability
- Lower credit rating
- Bankruptcy if business cannot obtain credit to meet its contractual financial obligations

See also INADEQUATE LIQUIDITY.

Problem: Inability to Issue New Securities

IDENTIFYING SYMPTOMS

- Investors refuse to deal in the company's new issuances of common stock, preferred stock, or bonds.
- The prices of existing securities drop significantly.
- Lenders place stringent credit requirements on the company.
- Financing costs increase.
- Previous sources of financing are no longer available.

CAUSES

- Market conditions
- Excessive business risk
- The quality of management
- Continuous operating losses
- Foreseeable negative future economic developments in the company's line of business
- Increased foreign competition

- Government action
- Excessive interest and labor costs
- Overexpansion or diversification into areas where the company has no experience
- Cash flow problems
- An overall deficient financial position
- Decline of company's stock and bond ratings

MEASUREMENT AND ANALYSIS. Examine the trend in the following ratios over the years and compare the company's ratios to those of competing companies and industry averages:

- Funds obtained from new bond financing to total liabilities
- Funds obtained from new stock financing to total stockholders' equity

REPAIR

- Give up greater control of the company to obtain funds.
- Try to place securities privately rather than publicly.
- Negotiate with venture capital groups.
- Provide collateral for financing.
- Seek out alternative financing strategies.
- Obtain open lines of credit from banks.
- Establish joint ventures with other companies to obtain financing.
- Offer higher financial incentives to investment bankers to encourage them to deal in the company's securities.
- Try to obtain government grants.
- Seek export financing in foreign countries.
- Delay capital expenditures.

PREVENTION TECHNIQUES

- Issue convertible exchangeable preferred stock that allows the company to force conversion from convertible preferred stock into convertible debt.
- Issue participating preferred stock that allows the shareholders to participate over and above the stated yield of the stock.

- Issue floating rate preferred stock.
- Offer Dutch auction preferred stock, in which the shares are reauctioned every seven weeks.
- Establish an Employee Stock Ownership Plan (ESOP) to place shares and votes in the friendly hands of employees.
- Issue new equity shares with preemptive rights.
- Institute an installment procedure whereby the company issues new securities over a stated period of time rather than all at once in one large offering.
- Time the issuance of new stocks and bonds to coincide with improving economic and market conditions.
- Issue shares in bull markets and refrain from issuing them in bear markets.
- Offer higher-yielding common stock just before the exdividend date so that investors will be attracted to it.
- Improve the internal generation of funds (cash flow from operations), so that there is less reliance on external financing.
- Improve the company's financial position through cost reduction programs and restructurings.
- Stretch repayment dates on bond issues.
- Refer to federal loan programs.

SPILLOVER EFFECTS.   The inability to issue new securities may create cash flow and operating problems:

- Increased cost of capital
- Higher compensating balances
- Increased business risk
- Financial instability
- Bankruptcy if business cannot obtain credit to meet its contractual financial obligations

If financing does become available, it may be at high risk and on very restrictive managerial terms. The financing restrictions will inhibit financial management's freedom of action.

A firm with a lower credit rating and a price per share may also become a candidate for takeover.

See also BANKRUPTCY LOOMS, BOND RATING DROPS, INABILITY TO REPAY DEBT, CASH OUTFLOWS EXCEED CASH INFLOWS, EXCESSIVE DEBT, INABILITY TO OBTAIN FINANCING, INADEQUATE CASH POSITION, INADEQUATE WORKING CAPITAL, INSOLVENCY, and POOR PROFITABILITY AND GROWTH.

Problem: Dividends Are Restricted

IDENTIFYING SYMPTOMS

- Cash flow problems
- Failure to generate earnings sufficient to pay a cash dividend
- Insolvency
- Loan agreements restricting the payment of dividends because a certain level of profits has not been attained
- Attempts to dismiss management by unhappy stockholders

CAUSES

- Insolvency
- Earnings too low to pay a cash dividend
- An urgent need (especially in rapidly growing businesses) for substantial funds to reinvest or finance investment opportunities
- Intentional failure by management to pay dividends because a majority of the shareholders are in a high marginal tax bracket (especially in cases where the company is a closely held corporation with few stockholders)
- Agreements in bond covenants with specific creditors requiring that a portion of the company's earnings be set aside as additional protection for creditors
- State laws requiring that accumulated earnings be restricted equal to the cost of treasury shares acquired
- Management desire to plow back earnings for financial growth or expansion
- Management decision to smooth out yearly dividend payments by accumulating earnings in profitable years and paying them out in years where there is an operating loss
- A policy of building up cash as a buffer against possible changes in the tax law or accounting rules, future tax audits, or operating losses

MEASUREMENT AND ANALYSIS. Dividends are payable only from funds legally available for such purposes under the law of the state of incorporation. Thus, the dividend yield (dividends per share/market price per share) is a measure of the current return to an investor in a stock. The dividend yield will drop if the corporation reduces or fails to pay a cash dividend for a given period of time.

Study the price/earnings (P/E) ratio. When a company's P/E ratio is higher than the P/E ratios of other companies, it usually signifies a potential for increased earnings and investor confidence because they expect high dividends and growth. On the other hand, a lower P/E ratio is usually the result of a negative assessment by investors. The payment of a stock dividend may also hide the inability of management to generate cash flow. The possibility may have a negative impact on sophisticated investors.

REPAIR

- Prepare a cash forecast to see whether the company can lift the restriction on the payment of cash dividends.
- Analyze the expansion requirements of the corporation.
- Attempt to maintain a pattern of consistent dividend payment.
- Seek to renegotiate agreements in bond covenants with specific creditors to reduce the requirement that a portion of the company's earnings be set aside as additional protection for creditors.

PREVENTION TECHNIQUES

- Pay a stock dividend or offer a stock split.
- Sell off unproductive assets or borrow funds to pay a cash dividend.

SPILLOVER EFFECTS.   The nonpayment or a reduction in the company's dividend payout ratio will cause a decline in the stock price. An added concern for a closely held company is the impact of changing dividends on stockholder personal tax liabilities.

Problem: Restrictive Loan Agreements Are Breached

IDENTIFYING SYMPTOMS

- Excessive debt
- Indications in a financial report that the agreed-upon ratios or limitations have been ignored by management
- Threats by creditors to demand payment of the entire amount outstanding, or to force the company into bankruptcy unless management reduces the outstanding debt back to the prior agreed-upon ratios, or rescinds the unauthorized transaction

CAUSES

- Demand for additional cash by management
- Failure by management to adhere to agreed-upon restraints in company loan procedures
- Misinterpretation or ignorance of the covenants found in the loan agreements

MEASUREMENT AND ANALYSIS.   Bondholders and other long-term creditors may exercise control through protective covenants in a loan agreement. Typical covenants include:

- A lower limit on the company's current ratio
- A minimum working capital requirement
- An upper limit on the company's debt/equity ratio
- A requirement that the enterprise not acquire or sell major assets over a stated amount without prior approval from the creditors
- A requirement that total loans shall not exceed a stated amount

REPAIR

- Hire an attorney and CPA to review all loan agreements.
- Have the accounting staff or outside auditors review the financial statements to make sure that they have been prepared correctly.
- Review the safety buffer between the loan requirement and actual financial status.
- Develop a professional and friendly relationship with the bank.
- Review all financial statements for accuracy in the recording of liabilities.
- Sell assets or issue additional shares of stock to pay off high-interest loans.
- Renegotiate loan restrictions to achieve greater flexibility in operations.
- Offer to exchange outstanding loan obligations for stock of the enterprise.

PREVENTION TECHNIQUES

- Reduce borrowing.
- Raise funds by issuing more stock.

- If a partnership, bring in additional partners who will provide additional funds.

SPILLOVER EFFECTS.   Increased loan interest costs or unavailability of financing, which may lead to excessive fixed costs and bankruptcy. The sale of stock may result in loss of control over the operation of the enterprise.

8

Risk
Overshadows
Return

There is a tradeoff between risk and return. The higher the risk, the greater should be the return. There are many corporate risks. A company may be overly dependent on a select few employees or government contracts, or there may be a militant union. Operations may be in politically and economically unstable foreign countries. Complex and burdensome environmental and safety regulations may apply to the company.

Many risks facing a business can be repaired, prevented, or eliminated because management can to some degree control them through such techniques as diversification, pricing strategies, and improved communication within the organization.

Problem: Disproportionate Risk to Return

IDENTIFYING SYMPTOMS

- Difficulty meeting debt payments
- Lower ratings on the company's stock and bond
- Inability to borrow or raise money on favorable terms

CAUSES

- Too much use of financial leverage (other people's money)
- Higher operating leverage caused by large fixed operating costs
- High debt/equity ratio
- High *beta* (the percentage change in the market price of the company's stock relative to the percentage change in the price of a stock index such as Standard & Poors 500)

MEASUREMENT AND ANALYSIS. The financial manager must compare the expected return for a given financial decision with the kind of risk involved. There are six separate types of risk:

1. *Business risk* is the risk that the company will have general business problems. It depends on changes in demand, input prices, and obsolescence due to technological advances.

2. *Liquidity risk* represents the possibility that an asset may not be sold on short notice for its market value. An investment that must be sold at a high discount is said to have substantial liquidity risk.

3. *Default risk* is the risk that the issuing company cannot make interest or principal repayments on debt.

4. *Market risk* refers to changes in the price of a stock that result from changes in the stock market as a whole, regardless of the fundamental change in a firm's earning power.

5. *Interest rate risk* refers to fluctuations in the value of an asset as the interest rates and conditions of the money and capital markets change. Interest rate risk relates to fixed income securities, such as bonds and real estate.

6. *Purchasing power risk* relates to the possibility of receiving less for an asset than was originally invested taking inflation into account.

REPAIR

- Monitor fixed discretionary operating costs (such as advertising and R&D).
- Pay off high-interest debts or exchange them for equity shares.

PREVENTION TECHNIQUES

- Balance the company's financing mix.
- Finance on favorable terms.
- Ensure that the company adheres to the "five C's": character, cash flow, capital, collateral, and economic condition.
- Keep bond ratings in a respectable category.

SPILLOVER EFFECTS

- A decline in the market value of the company, resulting in possible bankruptcy
- Difficulty obtaining financing on favorable terms
- Downgraded credit and bond ratings

See also BOND RATING DROPS, LOW RATE OF RETURN, POOR CREDIT RATING, and RISK IN CORPORATE OPERATIONS.

Problem: Risk in the Industry

IDENTIFYING SYMPTOMS. Industrywide, there are signs of contraction, turbulence, and vulnerability, as evidenced in:

- Declining sales and profitability
- A high degree of managerial turnover
- Overreliance on energy and a consequent vulnerability to energy shortage
- Stringent governmental and environmental regulation and unfavorable tax rules
- Consistently low marks in the *Wall Street Journal* and *Barron's*
- Continuous consumer lawsuits relating to product quality, performance, and environmental hazards
- A negative public image
- A growing vulnerability to new and improved products from both domestic and foreign competition

CAUSES

- There is excessive competition and/or a limited number of companies control a high percentage of the market.
- The companies in the industry cannot raise prices to meet increasing costs.
- The industry is technologically oriented and is having trouble fighting obsolescence and keeping up to date.
- The companies in the industry are capital-intensive, with a record of cyclical performance.

MEASUREMENT AND ANALYSIS

- Appraise the industry cycle.
- Evaluate the past and projected stability of the industry.

REPAIR

- Diversify by acquiring companies in growing and/or countercyclical industries.
- Acquire or merge with one or more competing companies.
- Move toward a labor-intensive business because it is easier to lay off employees in recessionary times than it is to reduce capital investment in plant and equipment.
- Move toward a staple-product business for greater earnings stability.

PREVENTION TECHNIQUES

- Diversify by acquiring companies in different industries and/or branching out into other product and service areas.

- Engage in joint ventures with other companies.

- Vertically integrate with energy suppliers.

- Cut product and service costs.

- Institute an advertising campaign to promote the industry's image.

- Settle consumer lawsuits out of court and establish a committee to review the causes of these actions.

- Lobby for legislation favorable to the industry.

SPILLOVER EFFECTS. Companies in an unhealthy industry tend to perform poorly. Excessive competition may result in declining profits and insolvency. The industry will lag in the stock market.

See also POLITICAL RISK.

Problem: Risk in Corporate Operations

IDENTIFYING SYMPTOMS

- Operations and earnings are unstable and consistently unprofitable.

- The company faces lawsuits for defective products, sexual harassment, etc.

- Upper management is unaware of existing or potential operating problems.

- The company has been the target of consumer boycotts and governmental intervention.

- There are contractual disputes with other companies and unions.

- The government is disputing certain contractual costs and is seeking to renegotiate existing contracts.

- There are tax problems with the Internal Revenue Service.

- There is a high turnover of experienced and valuable employees.

- Production quotas and schedules are not being met.

- Sales orders are not being filled because completed inventory is not available for immediate shipment.

- Costs are not being monitored.

- There are inadequate internal control procedures.

CAUSES

- Overdependence on a few key executives, unreliable suppliers, and a few large customers
- Improper hiring and training of employees
- Lack of a well-defined policy of corporate ethics and behavior
- Products and services that are susceptible to rapid technological change and obsolescence

MEASUREMENT AND ANALYSIS

- Compare a company's risk exposure to that of other companies in the industry and to the firm's past record.
- Use Beta to measure the company's risk relative to the market. Beta is the percentage change in the price of a company's stock to the percentage change in a stock market index (e.g., Dow Jones 30). A Beta greater than 1 means risk, because the company's stock vacillates more than the average.
- Evaluate labor quiescence by determining the number and duration of previous strikes, degree of union militancy, and employee turnover.
- Calculate operating and financial leverage. (*Operating leverage* is the percentage change in earnings before tax and interest to the percentage change in sales. *Financial leverage* is the ratio of total debt to total equity.)

REPAIR

- Develop a greater executive base.
- Change suppliers who prove unreliable.
- Diversify the customer base.
- Seek to improve labor relations.
- Improve communications between senior and operating managers.
- Settle disputes with all governmental agencies as quickly as possible.
- Review and evaluate internal control procedures for recording expenses.

PREVENTION TECHNIQUES

- Diversify products and investments.

- Move into new domestic and international markets. (However, avoid overexpanding where you lack expertise.)
- Acquire a successful existing company to obtain experienced management, new channels of distribution, sources of supply, economies of scale, and customer base.
- Diversify the current customer and supplier base.
- Develop a negative correlation between products and services.
- Enter countercyclical lines of business.
- Emphasize items with *inelastic demand* (demand that remains relatively stable, as with medicine, even though the price changes).
- Obtain adequate insurance for possible asset and operating losses.
- Improve hiring practices to obtain the most competent and productive employees.
- Establish employee programs that identify the kind of inappropriate employee behavior that might provoke lawsuits.
- Update employee skills.
- Improve community relations.
- Alter the geographic locations of operations to minimize such environmental risks as floods.
- Improve and review tax-planning techniques.

SPILLOVER EFFECTS

- Operating losses
- Lower market prices for the company's stocks and bonds
- More costly financing
- Difficulty hiring qualified and experienced personnel

See also DISPROPORTIONATE RISK TO RETURN, EXCESSIVE DEBT, EXCESSIVE OPERATING LEVERAGE, INFLATIONARY RISK, POLITICAL RISK, and RISK IN THE INDUSTRY.

Problem: Lack of Diversification

IDENTIFYING SYMPTOMS

- Increased risk
- Highly specialized and concentrated operations
- Lower profitability
- Low investment portfolio return

CAUSES

- Overreliance on a single product, with consequent susceptibility to revenue fluctuation and product obsolescence
- A product line with a high positive correlation and demand for all the products moving in one direction
- Products with elastic demand, experiencing significant changes in quantity with modest changes in price
- All company operations located in one geographic region and thus highly dependent on the economic and political makeup of that locality
- An investment portfolio concentrated in securities issued by industries involved in the same sectors of business

MEASUREMENT AND ANALYSIS.   In appraising a company's product line, determine:

1. The *degree of correlation* that exists between its products
2. The *elasticity of product demand*

The correlation between products is revealed through a correlation matrix determined by computer. The elasticity of a product's demand is measured by the percentage change in quantity sold associated with a percentage change in price.

The following ratio is used:

$$\frac{\text{Percentage change in quantity sold}}{\text{Percentage change in price}}$$

If the ratio is greater than 1, elastic demand is indicated. If it is exactly 1, demand is unitary. If the ratio is less than 1, inelastic demand exists. *Risk exists when products are positively correlated and have elastic demands.* This is because the demand for the products all moves in the same direction and product demand is significantly influenced by price changes.

Example 1:   The correlation matrix of company I's product line follows:

Product	A	B	C	D	E	F
A	1.0	.13	−.02	−.01	−.07	.22
B	.13	1.0	−.02	−.07	.00	.00
C	−.02	−.02	1.0	.01	.48	.13
D	−.01	−.07	.01	1.0	.01	−.02
E	−.07	.00	.48	.01	1.0	.45
F	.22	.00	.13	−.02	.45	1.0

Of course, perfect correlation exists with the same product. For example, the correlation between product A and product A is 1.0.

High positive correlation exists between products E and C (.48) and products E and F (.45). Since these products are *closely* tied to each other, risk is indicated.

Low negative correlation exists between products A and D (−.01) and products A and C (−.02).

No correlation exists between products B and E (.00) and products B and F (.00).

It would be better for company I if it had some products that had significant negative correlations (i.e., −.6). Unfortunately, it does not.

Example 2: The two major products of company J are X and Y. Data relevant to them follow:

	X	Y
Selling price per unit	$10.00	$8.00
Current sales in units	10,000	13,000

It is determined that if the selling price of product X is increased to $11.00, the sales volume will decrease by 500 units. If the selling price of product Y is increased to $9.50, the sales volume will decrease by 4000 units.

The elasticity of demand is:

$$\frac{\text{Percentage change in quantity sold}}{\text{Percentage change in price}}$$

Product X has inelastic demand:

$$\frac{500/10,000}{\$1/\$10} = \frac{.05}{.10} = .5$$

Product Y has elastic demand:

$$\frac{4,000/13,000}{\$1.50/\$8.00} = \frac{.307}{.188} = 1.63$$

Evaluate the degree of diversification and stability associated with the company's investment portfolio. Securities should be diversified by industry and economic sector.

REPAIR

- Immediately diversify by product line, geographic area, and investment securities.
- Set up a strategic unit to develop a diversification plan.

PREVENTION TECHNIQUES

- Diversify the product line to reduce the range of results that stem from differing economic conditions.

- Acquire established operating companies selling profitable products.

- Move from elastic product demand to inelastic product demand to enhance stability in operations and reduce risk.

- Diversify geographically to reduce risk of economic declines. This may be done regionally (among states and cities) or internationally (among countries).

- Diversify the investment portfolio to increase its price stability.

- Add international investments to a portfolio of U.S. securities.

SPILLOVER EFFECTS

- Greater uncertainty
- Decreased earning power
- Deteriorating growth rate
- More susceptibility to the shocks of the business cycle

Problem: Inflationary Risk

IDENTIFYING SYMPTOMS

- Real earnings are declining even though profitability seems satisfactory.

- Assets are losing purchasing power and/or are being improperly managed.

- Costs are escalating beyond control.

CAUSES

- The company is not keeping abreast of inflation by increasing the selling prices of its goods and services.

- Current prices for future deliveries are not guaranteed by futures contracts.

- Cost increases are not hedged.

- Monetary assets are losing purchasing power.

- The company is *not* adequately taking advantage of monetary liabilities that result in purchasing power gains during inflationary periods.

MEASUREMENT AND ANALYSIS. Determine the impact of inflation on net income by comparing the consumer price index (CPI) adjusted net income, and current cost net income with the reported earnings. If the amount reported in the income statement is materially higher than the other net income measure(s), the quality of earnings is poor. The wider the difference, the lower the quality of net income.

REPAIR

- Increase selling prices at short intervals to maintain adequate profit margins.
- Modify price catalogues and sales literature to reflect increases in prices of products and services.
- Give price quotations only for short periods of time (e.g., two months).
- Set sales pricing on a next-in, first-out basis.
- Include the current cost of capital in the selling price.
- Price ahead of inflation.
- Provide for price increases when there are long lead times between receiving orders and shipping goods.
- Obtain partial payments as work is performed.
- Have "cost plus" provisions, possibly tied to the Consumer Price Index, in long-term contracts.
- Enter into futures contracts to guarantee raw materials at currently lower prices.
- Restrict dividends to preserve earning power and retain needed cash.

PREVENTION TECHNIQUES

- Try to cut costs and improve efficiency.
- Substitute cheaper sources of supply or self-manufacture the part.
- Contract for long-term purchase agreements and encourage suppliers to quote firm prices.
- Look for suppliers who offer beneficial credit terms.
- Obtain competitive bids from insurance companies and periodically change carriers to secure the lowest premium charges.
- Redesign the delivery system to reduce fuel costs.
- De-emphasize inflation-resistant products.
- Avoid marketing proposals that require significant investments and have long payback periods.
- Tie salary increments to increased productivity.

- Keep cash and receivables at minimum balances because of a purchasing power loss.

- Use debt to gain purchasing power (because payments are made to creditors in cheaper dollars).

- Make investments in areas requiring minimal expenditures and short lead times.

- Use accounting methods that reduce taxable income so as to minimize tax payments.

SPILLOVER EFFECTS.   The failure to reduce inflation risk will erode the purchasing power of the company's dollars. In real dollars, the company is experiencing a diminishing economic position. The final result is an adverse effect on earnings, cash flow, and the company's stock price in the marketplace.

Problem: Political Risk

IDENTIFYING SYMPTOMS

- A long-term investment abroad
- Stringent governmental requirements

CAUSES

- Domestic spending on contracts and government subsidies is vulnerable to changing political realities.

- Agricultural enterprises are hurt by commodity embargoes.

- Government regulations are very stringent, thereby tying financial management's prerogatives.

- The company is vulnerable to current and proposed tax legislation that will result in increased taxes.

- A local regulatory body is hostile to the company.

- A utility's request for a rate increase is denied or delayed.

- There is a war in regions with high U.S. investment.

MEASUREMENT AND ANALYSIS.   Businesses tend to make long-term investments in foreign countries. Since it may take a long period of time to recover the initial investment, companies do not expect to liquidate their initial investment quickly. This situation generally produces difficulties in the repatriation of funds from a foreign country when the ruling government is subject to change. Compounding these difficulties are currency fluctuations and restrictive local customs and regulations. For example, a United States company doing business in Japan may be unable to fire employees making labor a fixed cost. There are also variations in tax laws, balance of payment policies, and government controls, with respect to the types and sizes of investments, along with the types of capital raised. Government controls may exist over wages, the selling price of the product or service, and local borrowing.

There may be stringent national and local environmental and safety regulations governing the manufacture of a product. An example of this is the expensive safety and pollution-control equipment mandated for new cars, an added production cost that cuts into the profitability of auto manufacturers.

International diversification of risks is an important motivation for foreign investment. Companies also invest in foreign countries to counter the investment actions of competitors. For example, if a manufacturing company establishes a factory in a foreign country, a competitor is likely to make a similar investment in the same country.

The financial manager of the multinational corporation (MNC) should determine and analyze the earnings derived and assets in each questionable foreign country. Useful ratios include:

Questionable foreign revenue to total revenue

Questionable foreign earnings to net income

Total export revenue to total revenue

Total export earnings to net income

Total assets in "questionable," or politically unstable foreign countries to total assets

Many MNCs and banks attempt to measure political risks in their businesses. They even hire or maintain a group of political risk analysts. Several independent services provide political risk and country risk ratings.

Country Risk Rating. This rating, put out annually by *Euromoney* magazine, is based on a measure of different countries' access to international credit, trade finance, political risk, and a country's payment record. The rankings are generally confirmed by political risk insurers and top syndicate managers in the Euromarkets.

Rating by *Economist Intelligence Unit.* This rating, by a New York–based subsidiary of the London *Economist Group,* is based on such factors as external debt and trends in the current account, the consistency of the government policy, foreign-exchange reserves, and the quality of economic management.

International Country Risk Guide. This rating is put out by a U.S. division of *International Business Communications,* Ltd., London, which offers a composite risk rating, as well as individual ratings for political, financial, and economic risk. The political variable—which makes up half the composite index—includes factors such as government corruption and how economic expectations diverge from reality. The financial rating looks at such things as the likelihood of losses from exchange controls and loan defaults. Finally, economic ratings consider such factors as inflation and debt-service costs.

Determine the percentage of earnings derived from government contract work and subsidies, and the degree to which such work and subsidies are of a recurring nature.

Determine the current and prospective effects of governmental interference on the company by reviewing current and proposed laws and regulations of governmental bodies as indicated in legislative hearings, trade journals, and newspapers.

REPAIR

- Investigate the current political status of the country where foreign operations are located.

- Establish a joint venture with a local entrepreneur.

- Purchase insurance when political risk in a foreign country is high.

  In the U.S., the Eximbank offers policies to exporters that cover such political risks as war, currency inconvertibility, and civil unrest. Furthermore, the Overseas Private Investment Corporation (OPIC) offers policies to U.S. foreign investors to cover such risks as currency inconvertibility, civil or foreign war damages, or expropriation.

  In the U.K., similar policies are offered by the Export Credit Guarantee Department (ECGD); in Canada, by the Export Development Council (EDC); and in Germany, by an agency called Hermes.

- Engage in forward exchange contracts to minimize exchange risk.

- Diversify across countries.

- Diversify into other activities that are not overly dependent on government business if operations are currently overly reliant on government contracts and subsidies.

- Lobby to influence legislators favorably disposed toward the company.

PREVENTION TECHNIQUES

- Evaluate the risk/return trade-off.

- Understand foreign country customs and laws before starting operations abroad.

- Hire consultants in the country where the foreign operations are to be located to assess the current political climate and to make contact with important officials to prevent any possible unforeseen political or operating problems.

- Establish a department (a mini State Department) to study and assess foreign political developments that may affect the company.

- Familiarize yourself with the domestic, local, and foreign regulatory environment in which the company and its subsidiaries operate.

- Use foreign brokers when specialized knowledge is needed.

- Try to promote a better relationship with unfriendly regulatory agencies.

- Establish a public relations program to counteract any proposed legislation that will adversely affect the company's earnings.

- Engage in sound tax planning to minimize taxes. Study foreign tax treaties to determine whether they contain beneficial provisions that your company can utilize to its advantage.

- Determine which foreign countries offer tax incentives to foreign companies establishing operations within their borders.

SPILLOVER EFFECTS

- Lower earning power and cash flow
- Negative impact on the market price of the company's stock and bonds
- Costly legal actions
- Adverse publicity
- Operating conditions so negative that the company is forced out of the country

See also DISPROPORTIONATE RISK TO RETURN and RISK IN CORPORATE OPERATIONS.

Problem: Foreign Exchange Risk

IDENTIFYING SYMPTOM.   There is an exchange risk from foreign currency transactions.

CAUSE.   Operations abroad, particularly in countries having significant fluctuation in exchange rates.

MEASUREMENT AND ANALYSIS.   A company may be exposed to foreign exchange risk when it participates in international markets.

Sales revenues may be collected in one currency, assets denominated in another, and profits measured in a third. Changes in exchange rates adversely affect sales by making competing imported goods cheaper.

The globalization of the world economy and the devaluation of the United States dollar have allowed many American companies to enter foreign markets. Speculative foreign currency exposure is due to a risk-prone financial management. The risk is caused by the fluctuation of the foreign currency exchange rate. The exposure to losses on purchase or sales commitments is the result of the foreign exchange contracts themselves.

Consider the exposed position of the firm in each foreign country in which there is a major operation. The degree of fluctuation of the foreign exchange rate may be measured by its percentage change over time and/or its standard deviation. Examine the trend in the ratio of foreign exchange gains and losses to net income and to total revenue. Determine the trend in losses on purchase and sales contracts over time.

REPAIR

- Forecast foreign exchange risks by considering:

  Recent rate movements
  Foreign inflation rate
  Balance of payments and trade
  Money supply growth
  Interest rate differentials

- Adopt a conservative foreign exchange posture.

- Bill customers in the company's reporting currency.

- Buy and sell forward exchange contracts in foreign currencies.

- Diversify and finance internationally.

PREVENTION TECHNIQUES

- Minimize transaction exposure by:

  1. Executing contracts in the forward exchange market or in the foreign exchange futures.
  2. Borrowing United States funds and investing the funds in securities of the country where the foreign credit purchase was made.

- Balance foreign assets and liabilities to protect the company from exchange rate fluctuations and profit variability.

- Operate only in those countries having stable rates.

- Establish foreign asset management programs that involve such strategies as switching cash and other currencies into strong currencies while piling up debt and other liabilities in depreciating currencies.
- Offer discounts to encourage quick collection in weak currencies.
- Offer liberal credit terms to customers paying in strong currencies.

SPILLOVER EFFECTS

- Excessive brokerage fees for executing foreign exchange contracts
- A decline in profitability and cash flow
- Investor uncertainty
- Accounting and tax problems

Problem: Social and Environmental Risks

IDENTIFYING SYMPTOMS

- Customers and the general public have a negative image of the business.
- Environmental conditions cause operating losses and shutdowns.
- The business causes pollution or creates hazardous waste.

CAUSES.   Social risk may be caused by:

- Strained ethnic, religious, sexual, age, and political conflicts
- Adverse or atypical weather conditions (particularly in the case of recreational businesses like resorts)
- An absence or breakdown of pollution control equipment mandating government intervention and fines

MEASUREMENT AND ANALYSIS.   Business enterprises have traditionally sought to maximize short-term profits while observing the minimal environmental protection required by law. The disregard of the environment by large corporations has now become a matter of public concern.

- Does the company have a reputation for employee discrimination?

- Is the company perceived as callous about public issues or the environment?
- Is worker safety of paramount importance?
- Has the federal government found violations of the Occupational Safety and Health Act (OSHA)?
- Does the company have a fair health insurance coverage plan for its workers?
- Is the business affected by the idiosyncracies of nature?

REPAIR

- Improve the company's image by putting more time and money into public relations.
- Hire local residents.
- Hire and promote more qualified minorities and women.
- Contribute to welfare and civic improvement programs.
- Sell marginally profitable operations that are the target of government regulation and environmental groups.
- Make worker safety a key company policy.
- Determine whether employee medical coverage is adequate.

PREVENTIVE TECHNIQUES

- Strictly enforce product quality control guidelines.
- Advertise in local newspapers to explain the company's support of community activities.
- Sponsor training workshops in low-employment areas, and hire qualified people who successfully complete the course.
- Settle discrimination cases out of court.
- Install new pollution-control facilities and upgrade existing ones.
- Reevaluate the firm's geographic location.

SPILLOVER EFFECTS

- Declining earning power
- Increased costs
- Lawsuits
- Fines

Problem: Management Unaware of Financial Problems

IDENTIFYING SYMPTOMS

- Costly inventory buildups
- Excessive production costs
- Operating inefficiencies
- Incompatible and uncoordinated programs

CAUSES

- Failure to consult with on-the-job personnel
- Failure to issue current, clear, or concise directives
- The issuing of too many memoranda
- Upper management belief that it can solve all financial and operating problems by itself

MEASUREMENT AND ANALYSIS.   Information about and communication of data are fundamental to controlling operations and reducing uncertainty and losses in any organization. Communications are essential to ensure that employees will carry out their necessary functions, thereby enabling the organization to meet its production goals, generate new ideas, and foster employee self-esteem and morale. A study should be made of the adverse financial effects of poor communication on company policy, major acquisitions or divestitures, or operating segments of the business.

REPAIR

- Have top management regularly consult with operating managers before making most decisions.
- Encourage top management to use various techniques for transmitting communications downward in the organization:

  Bulletin boards
  Regular meetings between upper managers, supervisors, and
      employees
  Company publications
  Payroll inserts

- Encourage communications by lower managers:

  Informal discussions with employees
  Exit interviews
  Discussions with union officials

Review of union grievances

Cash bonuses for valuable employee suggestions

"Communication sessions" in which employees are encouraged to fire questions at executives relating to the operations of the business

PREVENTION TECHNIQUES

- Make communications clear, concise, and as brief as possible.
- Ensure that there is straightforward and honest interaction among different levels of management.
- Review company developments in light of their impact on employees.
- Form a policy committee to establish and oversee an effective communications policy.

SPILLOVER EFFECTS.   Failure to adequately plan operating policy may result in:

- Declining profitability
- Cost inefficiencies
- Operating bottlenecks
- Possible bankruptcy

9

Budgeting and Forecasting Problems

If actual costs exceed expected costs, a business's profits will fall. If actual revenue is less than expected revenue, product quality or sales effort may be at fault. Differences between actual costs and budget signal inefficiencies that require immediate corrective action. Often, the problem is poor financial planning as reflected in erroneous and unrealistic budget figures. If sales and expense estimates are not reasonably reliable, the entire planning and control process can be put into question.

A company "will miss the mark" if it does not have the right product at the most opportune time. Poor use of manufacturing facilities will result in scheduling problems and cost overruns. Without adequate financial resources, the company cannot grow.

Problem: Actual Costs Exceed Budgeted Costs

IDENTIFYING SYMPTOMS

- A lack of available funds toward the end of the accounting period
- A consistently too-tight budget estimate that no one can realistically meet
- Significant differences between budget and actual expenditures

CAUSES

- Inexperienced management
- A lack of cost control and planning
- A lack of efficiency and cost management
- Experimental or "pet" projects that do not meet the company's profit goals
- Duplication of effort and facilities
- Waste

- Budgets based solely on historical experience instead of current operating environment
- Use of a static (fixed) budget geared for only one level of activity

MEASUREMENT AND ANALYSIS. The difference (variance) between budgeted cost and actual cost for each major product line item should be examined over an operating period. The reason and party responsible for the deviation should be determined, and corrective steps undertaken.

Flexible budgeting differentiates between fixed and variable costs, thus allowing for a budget that can be automatically adjusted (through changes in variable-cost totals) to the particular level of activity *actually* attained. Thus, variances between actual costs and budgeted costs are adjusted for volume ups and downs before differences due to price and quantity factors are computed.

The flexible budget as opposed to the static budget can help provide accurate measurements of performance by comparing actual costs for a given output with the budgeted costs for the *same level of output.* A flexible budget is geared toward a range of activity rather than a single level of activity, and it is dynamic, rather than static: a series of budgets can be developed for various activity levels.

REPAIR

- Implement a cost-reduction program to trim excessive expenditure.
- Restructure and reorganize to reduce "fat" in the organization and make the company leaner and more efficient.
- Eliminate duplicate activities and facilities.
- Merge operations to generate cost efficiencies.
- Consolidate facilities and equipment to achieve a more efficient productivity level.
- Subcontract out some work at a lower cost.
- Obtain union concessions to reduce wages and fringe benefits or to increase productivity.
- Evaluate leased premises to reduce rental charges. (Closely examine square footage prices, commercial rent tax, and escalation clauses.)
- Cut back on travel costs by using conference calls and video teleconferences.
- Enter into joint ventures to cut costs and eliminate duplications.
- Implement an energy-conservation program.
- Identify variances early in the evaluation process.

- If variances are due to poor estimation, improve the budgeting process.
- Obtain more favorable credit terms from suppliers.

PREVENTION TECHNIQUES

- Formulate a cost-control program.
- Place "caps" on expense categories (such as travel and entertainment) requiring special permission to exceed maximum amounts.
- Reduce advertising and promotional expense.
- Assign each employee an identification number for xerox, fax, and computer use to prevent abuse.
- Undertake an engineering study to see if manufactured items can be redesigned to save costs.
- Use financial models to include all relevant variances in budgetary estimates.
- Use a flexible budget.

SPILLOVER EFFECTS

- Earnings will significantly fall off.
- Overall business operations will be deficient and productivity will be adversely affected.
- Future planning and direction will be inaccurate.

See also ACTUAL COSTS EXCEED STANDARD COSTS and INADEQUATE COST CONTROLS.

Problem: Actual Costs Exceed Standard Costs

IDENTIFYING SYMPTOMS

- Excess costs
- Manufacturing delays
- Inefficient budgeting
- Waste
- Idle production facilities
- A wide difference between production and sales
- Inferior quality of manufactured goods

CAUSES

- Actual costs exceed standard costs because of managerial ineffectiveness.

- Standards are out-of-date or inaccurate because of poor budgetary estimation.

- Price (rate, spending) variances are unfavorable, due to price increases and a lack of proper cost control.

- Quantity (usage) variances are unfavorable, due to poor quality of materials, lack of supervision, and incompetent workers.

- Production volume is consistently unfavorable, due to inadequate facilities, inefficient scheduling, lack of orders, defective raw materials, incorrect tooling, lack of employee productivity, machine breakdowns, long operating times, and/or failure to obtain raw materials on time.

MEASUREMENT AND ANALYSIS.   A *standard cost* is the predetermined cost of manufacturing an item during a given future production period. An *unfavorable cost variance* indicates that actual costs exceed standard costs. Variances can be arrived at only when the actual figures are known at the end of the production period. When a product is produced or a service is performed, the following three measurements must be determined:

1. *Actual cost.*   This equals actual price times actual quantity, where actual quantity equals actual quantity per unit of work times actual units of work produced.

2. *Standard cost.*   This equals standard price times standard quantity, where standard quantity equals standard quantity per unit of work times actual units of work produced.

3. *Total (control) variance.*   This equals actual cost less standard cost. Total (control) variance has the following elements.

Price (rate, spending) variance

$$= \text{(standard price} - \text{actual price)} \times \text{actual quantity}$$

Quantity (usage, efficiency) variance

$$= \text{(standard quantity} - \text{actual quantity)} - \text{standard price}$$

These are computed for both material and labor. A variance is unfavorable when actual cost is higher than standard cost.

REPAIR

- Improve the budgeting process.

- Institute a cost-reduction program.
- Pinpoint the party or parties responsible.
- To correct an unfavorable material price variance, increase the selling price, substitute cheaper materials, change a production method or specification, engage in a cost-reduction program, and combine overall resources.
- To repair an unfavorable labor efficiency situation, buy better machinery, revise plant layout, improve operating methods, and upgrade employee training and development.
- Improve the volume variance through better scheduling and supervision.
- Make volume purchases when discounts are attractive.
- Perform inspection at key points in the manufacturing cycle.

PREVENTION TECHNIQUES

- Standards should be modified when they no longer reflect current conditions.
- Use the "management-by-exception" principle to highlight problem areas.
- Computerize variance reporting for immediate feedback and analysis.
- Adjust output levels.
- Evaluate the purchasing department to assure that it is obtaining the best possible material at the least possible price.
- Emphasize vertical integration to reduce the price and supply risk of raw materials.
- Perform maintenance on a regular basis to improve the functioning of machinery.
- Improve employees' knowledge and efficiency.

SPILLOVER EFFECTS. A lack of cost control will result in an item at a higher cost that does not meet predetermined standards. Unfavorable cost variances (and resultant higher selling prices) will lead to less competitiveness in the marketplace and less profitability because of excessive costs. Unless these costs are controllable in the future, business failure may occur.

See also ACTUAL COSTS EXCEED BUDGETED COSTS and INADEQUATE COST CONTROLS.

Problem: Actual Revenue Below Standard Revenue

IDENTIFYING SYMPTOMS

- Reduced selling price
- Decline in sales volume and market share
- Increase in sales returns
- Advertising ineffectiveness

CAUSES

- Sales price variance is unfavorable because the product is being sold at a discount.
- A sales volume variance is unfavorable because of an inaccurate standard, poor sales effort, and loss of market position.
- Sales are unfavorable because of poor quality.

MEASUREMENT AND ANALYSIS

The total sales variance

$$= \text{expected sales revenue} - \text{actual sales revenue}$$

The total sales variance should be separated into price and volume. Each should then be analyzed for the reasons behind the variance.

Sales price variance

$$= (\text{actual selling price} - \text{budgeted selling price}) \times \text{actual units sold}$$

Sales volume variance

$$= (\text{actual quantity} - \text{budgeted quantity}) \times \text{budgeted selling price}$$

The sales variances are computed to gauge the performance of the marketing function.

Examine salesperson variances to determine the effectiveness of the salesforce by looking at cost and time spent. The salesperson variances are determined as follows:

$$\text{Total cost variance} = \text{actual cost} - \text{standard cost}$$

Variance in salesperson days

$$= (\text{actual days} - \text{standard days}) \times \text{standard rate per day}$$

Variance in salesperson costs

$$= (\text{actual rate} - \text{standard rate}) \times \text{actual days}$$

Total variance in calls $= (\text{actual calls} - \text{actual sale})$

$$\text{vs. } (\text{standard calls} - \text{standard sale})$$

Variance in calls = (actual calls − standard calls) × standard sale

Variance in sales = (actual sale − standard sale) × standard calls

Joint variance

   = (actual calls − standard calls) × (actual sale − standard sale)

REPAIR

- Improve sales planning and forecasting.
- Improve product quality, design, packaging, or sales mix if necessary.
- Dispose of out-dated styles and slow-moving stock.
- Identify who is responsible for sales variances and take corrective action.
- Increase prices if the market will bear it.
- To stimulate sales, offer better services, launch as many new products as possible, offer sales promotions, provide rebates, offer discounts, and give zero percent financing.

PREVENTION TECHNIQUES

- If the total sales variance is unfavorable, concentrate on the marketing aspects, since the variance indicates a problem with sales, advertising, and pricing.
- Use computerized software, such as spreadsheets, to determine sales variances by major product.
- Keep track of salesperson costs and compare them to budgeted figures.
- Pay higher commission rates to salespeople to promote high-profit margin items and slow-moving ones.

SPILLOVER EFFECTS.   If revenue is less than expected, the business will be less profitable than anticipated. A decline in the revenue base may result in layoffs and other cost-cutting measures. The survival of a business is questionable if sales continue to slide.

Problem: Inaccurate Sales and Expense Estimates

IDENTIFYING SYMPTOM.   Projected costs are substantially different from actual expenditures.

CAUSES

- Computational errors
- Incorrect application of budgetary procedures
- Incorrect forecasting of variables to which specific revenues or expenditures are related
- Failure to anticipate unusual occurrences, such as uninsured catastrophes
- Intentional overestimating of projected expenditures to enhance the appearance of superior performance
- Intentional overestimating of revenues to satisfy current and potential investors and creditors
- Failure to consult with the managers of specific performance centers
- Failure to use up-to-date, sophisticated forecasting models that include all explanatory variables
- Lack of careful planning

MEASUREMENT AND ANALYSIS.   Actual revenues and actual expenses should be compared to estimated revenues and estimated expenses. If significant differences exist over time, the budgetary process is deficient. The reasons for the discrepancies should be analyzed and corrective action taken.

REPAIR

- Analyze the preparation of the budget.
- Compare budgeted figures to actual figures.
- Include departmental and sales managers in the process.
- Use experienced staff and budgeting software to prevent mathematical errors.

PREVENTION TECHNIQUES

- Improve the company's forecasting procedures.
- Include marketing and production managers, financial planners, and accountants in the planning process.
- Use forecasts that take into account the economic environment in which the business operates.
- Use financial planning models in the forecasting process to take into account all the variables affecting the estimates.

SPILLOVER EFFECTS

- Deficient budgeting reflects a general lack of careful planning, control, and direction by management.

- Inaccurate predictions of future revenue and expenses result in inefficient planning and unsubstantiated decision making that can negatively affect company performance, growth, and profitability.

- Inaccurate sales projections result in inaccurate production estimates and to the hiring of either too many or too few employees.

- If sales estimates are off, the expected production volume will also be incorrect, which can lead to excessive buildup in inventory and exposure to possible future inventory write-offs because of obsolescence.

- Manufacturing costs will be exceptionally high and nonproductive.

See also ACTUAL COSTS EXCEED BUDGETED COSTS.

Problem: Lack of the Right Product at the Right Time

IDENTIFYING SYMPTOMS

- New products fail because of lack of customer demand.
- Products are introduced at inopportune times.

CAUSES

- High competition
- Poor marketing
- Insufficient planning
- Inadequate production budget
- Poor product design

MEASUREMENT AND ANALYSIS

- Compute the ratio of failed products to total products.
- Determine why a product failed, what losses have occurred, and who was responsible.
- Analyze the product's research and development costs.

REPAIR

- Advertise to improve customer demand.
- Strengthen sales efforts.

PREVENTION TECHNIQUES

- Market analysis of consumer demands
- Product planning and analysis
- Cost feasibility studies

SPILLOVER EFFECTS

- The business will lose money.
- The company's growth rate will decline.
- Customers will lose faith in the product.
- The overall reputation of the business will suffer.

Problem: Poor Use of Production Capacity

IDENTIFYING SYMPTOMS

- Increasing manufacturing expenditures
- Downtime
- Failure to meet production schedules
- Poor-quality manufactured goods
- Increased repairs

CAUSES

- Poor production planning and analysis
- Poor supervision, design, and scheduling by engineers
- Obsolete and malfunctioning equipment
- Failure to test operations on a random basis
- Inexperienced or incompetent workers
- Purchase of the wrong equipment
- Failure to use quantitative techniques such as *linear programming* (allocation of limited resources to maximize gain and minimize cost)

MEASUREMENT AND ANALYSIS. The measures which may be used to evaluate the inefficiency of productive capacity are:

- Number and length of machine breakdowns
- Output per man-hour
- Input-output relationship (what was put in, in terms of time and money, versus what was put out, in terms of quantity and quality)
- The trend in the ratio of manufacturing costs to total costs and to revenue
- The trend in the ratio of indirect to direct labor hours
- The trend in the ratio of repairs and maintenance to the carrying value of equipment
- The number and duration of manufacturing delays and backlog of orders
- Variances between budget and actual production volume and costs

Compute the trend in the ratio of indirect labor to direct labor. The ratio monitors indirect manpower planning and control. A declining trend is unfavorable because it indicates that management has *not* maintained a desirable relationship between indirect labor and direct personnel.

Determine the operating assets ratio (operating assets to total assets). A decline in the ratio means worsening operations and production capacity. The operating ratio concentrates on those assets *actively employed in current operations.* Such assets exclude past-oriented assets and future-oriented assets. Past-oriented assets arise from prior errors, inefficiencies, or losses because of competitive factors or changes in business plans. These assets have not yet been formerly recognized in the accounts. Examples are obsolete goods, idle plants, receivables under litigation, delinquent receivables, and nonperforming loans (no interest being recognized). Future-oriented assets are acquired for corporate growth or generating future sales. Examples are land held for speculation and factories under construction. Nonoperating assets reduce profits and return on investment because no benefit to current operations occurs. They neither generate sales nor reduce costs. Rather, they are a "drain" on the company and may require financing.

Compare sales dollars and/or sales volume to the number of employees and/or salaries as an indicator of employee productivity. Low ratios mean a lack of revenue derived from employee time spent and payroll incurred. Thus manpower is not being used productively.

REPAIR

- Track down and replace those responsible for the poor use of manufacturing facilities.

- Subcontract work.
- Increase inspection at key points in the manufacturing process.
- Maintain productive assets and replace obsolete fixed assets.
- Improve employee training and morale.

PREVENTION TECHNIQUES

- Replace obsolete and ineffective machinery.
- Improve training and instruction in machine use.
- Improve coordination among all parties involved in manufacturing.

SPILLOVER EFFECTS

- Increased operating costs
- Lower profits
- Manufacturing delays
- Machinery breakdowns

See also EXCESSIVE COST-TO-PRODUCTION VOLUME.

Problem: Expansion Exceeds Financial Resources

IDENTIFYING SYMPTOMS

- No funds available for sustained capital growth
- Capital expenditures must be reduced because of the delay in receiving debt and equity funds

CAUSES

- A shortage in the money supply
- Poor economic conditions
- Deficient corporate financial health
- Industry problems
- Growth that outstrips the company's financial resources
- Lower credit rating
- Risky projects undertaken with inadequate cash resources

MEASUREMENT AND ANALYSIS.   Evaluate the trend in the ratio of capital expansion to dollar financing obtained. A high ratio may mean that investment in property, plant, and equipment is not adequately supported by outside funds. Restrictions placed on the use of funds by lenders may indicate apprehension about a company's capital investments. The ratio of debt to assets will also indicate the amount of debt incurred to obtain assets.

REPAIR

- Cut back on expansion or obtain additional financing.
- Enter into joint ventures to obtain financial backing.

PREVENTION TECHNIQUES

- Improve planning for the acquisition of capital facilities.
- Reduce expansion efforts.
- Secure new lines of credit.
- Synchronize cash outlays to cash inflows.
- Undertake joint ventures with other enterprises.
- More accurately forecast the demand for capital expenditures.

SPILLOVER EFFECTS.   If the business expands without the required financial support, it may be unable to complete its proposed projects. These may become nonproductive assets that tie up corporate resources without obtaining adequate return, a situation that will result in declining profitability or operating losses.

10

Noncompetitive Compensation

Financial problems result when employees are overcompensated in salaries and fringe benefits, including pension and health care. Compensation should be tied to productivity. A business cannot stay afloat if its labor costs are more than the value of its employee output. An obvious indication of danger occurs when employee labor hours and costs are increasing while production volume is decreasing. A declining trend in revenue per employee (sales divided by the number of employees) is another ominous sign. Management must immediately correct quality problems in manufactured goods due to inferior workmanship and should also examine employee turnover, absences, and slowdowns.

Problem: Low Financial Incentive for Employee Productivity

IDENTIFYING SYMPTOMS

- High absenteeism and turnover
- Escalating incentive costs but no consequent reduction in employee absenteeism and turnover

CAUSES

- Low pay
- Inadequate or nonexistent fringe benefit package

MEASUREMENT AND ANALYSIS. Effective compensation administration is essential to increase employee satisfaction. The compensation should be adequate, equitable, balanced, and cost effective. It should provide both an incentive for satisfactory job performance and reward for productive work. A fringe benefits package may include stock option and bonus plans, pension and profit-sharing plans, group life insurance, hospitalization and medical plans, and death payments. Despite the escalating costs of fringe benefits, financial management has no choice but to offer them.

REPAIR

- Develop a compensation and incentive budget.
- Try to create new plans that employees want.
- Hire a compensation and incentive benefits expert. After comparing its own compensation and fringe benefits costs to those of other firms with the aid of data from an industry or professional group or sources such as the Chamber of Commerce, the organization should attempt to at least match the compensation and incentive plans offered by other employers.
- Provide for no-cost or low-cost benefits. A "no-additional-cost service" is a service provided by the employer to an employee or employee's spouse or dependents for which the employer incurs no substantial additional cost. (For example, airlines provide discount stand-by tickets to employees and their families.)
- Develop a deferred-compensation plan whereby employees can defer compensation and any applicable taxes until retirement.

PREVENTION TECHNIQUES

- Set objectives for the compensation strategy.
- Involve participants and unions in the benefits program.
- Tell employees about the benefits package.
- Monitor all financial costs.
- Encourage employees to participate in deciding what benefits they should be offered.

SPILLOVER EFFECTS. A lack of adequate financial compensation for employee productivity will result in morale problems, less employee cooperation, decreased productivity, strikes, and turnover.

Problem: Unfunded Retirement Benefits

IDENTIFYING SYMPTOMS

- Cash flow problems
- Failure to meet funding requirements
- Failure to make fund contributions

CAUSES

- Poor management
- Extravagant funding requirements
- Generous ancillary benefits
- Erroneous actuarial assumptions

MEASUREMENT AND ANALYSIS.   Virtually all qualified retirement plans entail significant costs to the employer. Pension plans, including defined benefit and money purchase plans, require a certain level of annual funding. Contributions are made from time to time to a trustee or insurance company which invests the funds until employees are entitled to receive distributions at retirement. The amount and timing of the contribution is determined by the specific type of plan. In addition, certain plans must pay insurance premiums to the Pension Benefit Guaranty Corporation (PBGC), a government agency that ensures that the level of benefits will be available to retirees even if the employer-funded trust is insufficient.

REPAIR

- Use outside auditors to review, on a monthly basis, the adequacy of the funded amounts.
- Hire a pension trustee to report any discrepancies or deviation from fund requirements to top management.
- Hire an actuary to determine whether the actuarial assumptions used to fund the plan are computed correctly.
- Try to amend the plan.
- Reduce ancillary benefits.
- Restrict such compensation bonuses and commissions.
- Seek to extend the time for filing the company's tax return. This extension will also serve as an extension for making a contribution to the pension plan. For example, a calendar-year employer with a pension plan can, for 1992, make a contribution by September 15, 1993, and avoid a funding deficiency.
- Pay costly administrative expenses from plan assets.
- Make contributions in property other than cash.
- Terminate "overfunded" defined benefit plans.
- Cut total payroll costs by reducing the workforce.
- Set up plans that can be funded exclusively with employee salary deferrals without employer contributions.

PREVENTION TECHNIQUES

- Continual audit by outside auditors to prevent the unauthorized use of pension funds

- A pension committee chosen from among the corporate directors (or from among the partners if a partnership) to oversee the proper operating and funding of the pension plan

- An investment manager to manage, acquire, or dispose of plan assets

SPILLOVER EFFECTS.   An employer who fails to meet funding requirements may incur liabilities to the retirement plan, the Internal Revenue Service, the Pension Benefit Guaranty Corporation (PBGC), and the Department of Labor for the continuing obligation of funding the plan. The employer may be sued by a plan participant to enforce its obligation to make the required employer contribution.

According to new accounting rules of the Financial Accounting Standards Board, a company must now record costs associated with postretirement health care benefits in the years in which employee services are performed. Many companies have had inadequate provisions on their books. As a result, huge expense and liability provisions may have to be recorded with significantly adverse effects on reported net income and balance-sheet position, including a drastic decline in earnings from the charge-off, reduction in cash flow to make up for previous underfunding of the plan, and increased debt recognition.

See also EXCESSIVE LABOR COSTS.

Chapter

11

Sales and Advertising Miss Margins

A business has a serious financial problem when its sales base is eroding. Advertising is not effective when it does not generate sales dollars. The problem can become acute when a lowered selling price actually shrinks profit margins because of rising costs. A high level of product returns means customer dissatisfaction and a loss in current and future business. A business cannot survive for long with a negative reputation. Management must also rethink its policy of increasing product or service pricing when either one causes sales to fall off.

Problem: Unprofitable Advertising Expenditures

IDENTIFYING SYMPTOM. Increased advertising expenditures with flat or declining sales.

CAUSES

- Poor planning by the marketing department
- Poor economic conditions that make consumers reluctant to spend
- Inaccurate or incompetent advertising

MEASUREMENT AND ANALYSIS. Advertising effectiveness should be measured and controlled. A comparison should be made over time using the ratios of advertising to sales, and advertising to net income. A higher ratio may indicate advertising ineffectiveness because advertising costs are being incurred without a significant impact on sales volume.

- Look at the sales and profit before, during, and after an advertising effort. If a particular campaign does not increase sales, it is a failure.

- Examine media surveys to determine whether your advertising is reaching your target audience in sufficient numbers.
- Determine whether advertising dollars are being spent in accordance with established company policy.
- Analyze the trends in company advertising efforts over time relative to those of competing companies within the industry.

REPAIR

- Analyze why an advertising campaign is not working and then eliminate or improve it.
- Determine if sales are down because of high pricing, and then reduce the selling price.

PREVENTION TECHNIQUES

- Undertake a careful and thorough marketing study to find the best way of advertising to reach the targeted audience.
- Do a cost/benefit analysis before the advertising campaign begins to assure that the campaign is worth the expense.
- Carefully appraise what the competition is doing.

SPILLOVER EFFECTS.   If advertising expenditures do not generate sufficient revenue, the excessive costs incurred will result in lower profitability.

Problem: Revenue Base Erosion

IDENTIFYING SYMPTOMS

- A decline in sales and other sources of revenue
- A loss in market share to competitors
- Selling prices marked down
- Products reaching the final stage of their cycle (down stage)
- Patented new products failing to appear
- A lack of overall customer demand, interest, and confidence
- Loss of a major customer
- A deteriorating reputation

CAUSES

- A poor economic environment
- A poor product mix
- A saturated market because of oversupply, competition, or technological obsolescence
- No new opportunities
- A high-risk product line
- Disappearing export sales

MEASUREMENT AND ANALYSIS

- Determine the trend in sales and nonoperating income sources over the last ten years. Compute the trend in the ratio of sales to net income and the ratio of nonoperating income to net income. Declining ratios are cause for concern.
- Determine the trend in a company's replacement and maintenance revenue as a percentage of (1) new sales; (2) total revenue; and (3) net income. Decreasing trends indicate eroding revenue.
- Determine the percentage of short-lived income to total revenue and net income. A high ratio indicates a future decline in revenue.
- Determine the variability in volume, price, and cost of each major product.
- Determine revenue derived from growth, mature, declining, and developmental products. A high percentage of declining and developmental products is a negative sign.
- Analyze the sales backlog to monitor sales status and planning.

REPAIR

- Diversify the product line and customer base.
- Expand abroad.
- Develop products whose sales will generate further sources of revenue. (An example is Xerox, which provides maintenance services and replacement parts to its customers.)
- Reduce risk in the product line.
- Establish joint ventures with foreign companies to maintain overseas markets.

PREVENTION TECHNIQUES

- Keep current with the latest technological developments.
- Engage in long-term contracts to assure steady business.

- Enter countercyclical lines of business to insulate yourself from economic cycles.

- Manufacture or buy products whose cost and price are stable.

- Introduce new products on an ongoing basis to replace existing ones that are losing their market appeal.

- Acquire competitors to gain more control of market conditions.

- Develop a product line of low-priced goods that can substitute for higher-priced goods and provide a built-in hedge against inflation and recession.

- Develop a piggyback product base (similar products all associated with the company's prime product or base business).

SPILLOVER EFFECTS.   An eroding revenue base will negatively affect future sales and profitability. The business may experience serious liquidity problems because of a lackluster performance and consequent lack of cash inflow.

See also ACTUAL REVENUE BELOW STANDARD REVENUE, PRODUCT REFINEMENT GENERATES A LOSS, and WEAK SALES MIX.

Problem: Higher Prices Reduce Sales

IDENTIFYING SYMPTOMS

- Customers shift to lower-priced items in the product line or switch to a competitor's product.

- Customers complain about the higher price.

CAUSES

- A recession causes consumers to watch their spending.

- Customers are reluctant to pay more for a product.

MEASUREMENT AND ANALYSIS.   A reduction in sales volume when the selling price is increased means that the product demand may be elastic. Determine the elasticity of the product to see the effect on volume as selling price is changed. (*See* LACK OF DIVERSIFICATION for an illustration of this computation.)

Determine the effect on profit at different selling prices by using a "what-if" spreadsheet analysis on Lotus 1-2-3 or other similar software program. Which selling price results in the best overall profit?

Assuming idle capacity, which is typically the case, total fixed cost remains the same with declining sales volume resulting in an increase in fixed cost per unit. While total variable costs will decline as production decreases, the variable cost per unit will be the same.

REPAIR

- Establish an appropriate price for a product or service based on costs, desired markup, capacity, supply/demand relationship, and competitive factors.

- Attempt to sell at a lower price to determine its effect on volume.

- Attempt to move toward inelastic products where a change in selling price will not affect volume.

- Promote the quality and reliability of the company's products and services.

- Attempt to market a substitute product that can be sold for less.

PREVENTION TECHNIQUES

- Redesign the product to reduce manufacturing costs, so that it can be sold at the same price.

- Try to reduce material, labor, and overhead costs, so that prices don't have to be increased (or don't have to be increased any further).

- Test-market the product at different selling prices to see which price is more attractive to consumers.

- Use a simulation model (a "what-if" model) to estimate the effects of alternative selling price changes on sales volume.

SPILLOVER EFFECTS

- The profitability of the business may remain flat or even decline.

- Customer loyalty to the company's other products may diminish.

- The company's market share and ability to maintain future operations may decline.

See also PRICING LOWERS PROFITS.

Problem: Lowered Prices Shrink Margins

IDENTIFYING SYMPTOMS

- The reduced price reduces the firm's profit margin (net income/sales).

- The reduced price increases sales volume, but the profit margin on each item sold is less.

CAUSES.   A lowered selling price may be needed to:

- Meet sluggish consumer demand, particularly in recessionary times
- Reduce a buildup in inventory of slow moving items
- Encourage customers to buy additional items in the product line
- Attract new customers
- Retain old customers

MEASUREMENT AND ANALYSIS.   A business should accept an order at below-normal price when:

- Idle capacity exists (since fixed cost remains constant), as long as there is a *contribution margin* on the order. (The contribution margin = price less variable costs.)
- The company is in financial distress.
- The firm is in a competitive bidding situation.

Example: Ten thousand units are currently sold at $30 per unit. Variable cost per unit is $18, and fixed costs total $100,000. Therefore, the fixed cost per unit equals $10 ($100,000/10,000). Idle capacity exists. A prospective customer is willing to buy 100 units at a selling price of only $20 per unit.

Ignoring market considerations (for example, unfavorable reaction by customers paying $30 per unit), you should recommend the sale of the additional 100 units. Why? Because it results in a positive additional (marginal) profitability of $200, as indicated in the following instance.

Sales (100 × $20)	$2000
Less variable cost (100 × $18)	(1800)
Contribution margin	200
Less fixed cost	0*
Net income	$ 200

*Because of idle capacity, there is no additional fixed cost. If the order were to increase fixed cost by $50, say, because it required a special tool, it is still financially advantageous to sell the item at $20. The additional profit is now $150, as illustrated in the next instance.

Sales (100 × $20)	$2000
Less variable cost (100 × $18)	(1800)
Contribution margin	200
Less fixed cost	(50)
Net income	$150

REPAIR

- Reduce the variable costs to maintain the same profit margin.
- Reduce manufacturing costs through redesign, cutting quality, reducing size, and so on.
- Reduce discretionary fixed costs (e.g., advertising, research and development).

PREVENTION TECHNIQUES.   Use contribution margin analysis to determine when the selling price can be lowered without eliminating the business's incremental profitability. The rule of thumb is to accept an order below the normal price if there is a contribution margin to cover the total fixed costs.

SPILLOVER EFFECTS.   A reduction in selling price leads to a lower profit per sales dollar. Customers who bought at the higher price may resent the price reduction. Therefore, the business should try to minimize the pain by referring to what happened as a discount sale, rebate, closeout, and so on.

See also PRICING LOWERS PROFITS.

Problem: High Level of Merchandise Returns

IDENTIFYING SYMPTOMS

- Customer complaints
- Loss of customers
- Returned delivery charges paid by the seller
- Government investigation for consumer fraud
- Having to give customers incentives to keep merchandise

CAUSES

- Poor quality merchandise
- Incorrect or excessive pricing
- Failure to meet specifications
- Delivery problems
- Deceptive advertising

MEASUREMENT AND ANALYSIS

- Investigate the trend in the ratio of sales returns and allowances to sales. An increasing trend indicates customer dissatisfaction.

- Compare the original selling price and the final discounted selling price. Is the final selling price the result of competition, defects in the product, design obsolescence, or other problems?

- Prepare a returned-materials report for each transaction. A written report describing the materials and why they are being returned should accompany materials being put back into stock.

REPAIR. To encourage customers not to return goods:

- Offer sales discounts.
- Provide free in-home service to correct problems.
- Improve packaging and shipping to minimize damage in delivery.
- Change unreliable delivery services.
- Install an 800 telephone hot-line number for dissatisfied customers.
- Offer other free merchandise as a bonus.
- Give credits toward future purchases.
- Use new and unique styles.

Take immediate action on quality problems. Check quality at each phase of the production process rather than just waiting until the finished product appears.

PREVENTION TECHNIQUES. Returns may be prevented by:

- Closely adhering to consumer laws
- Implementing a total quality management (TQM) system
- Using higher-quality materials and components for manufactured goods
- Increasing inspection of goods before shipment
- Improving billing procedures
- Double-checking physical counts
- Having legal staff check advertising
- Dropping products with an above-average complaint and defect rate
- Using public relations programs to promote the image of the company

- Checking to ensure that products meet customer requirements
- Surveying letters of complaint from dealers and customers
- Testing new products for reliability and performance
- Asking employees why products have quality problems

SPILLOVER EFFECTS

- Declining sales and profits
- Loss of future business
- Criminal or civil lawsuits arising from product liability or false advertising
- Consumer boycotts
- A long-lasting negative image or reputation

12

Weak Internal Controls

A business with a weak internal control structure cannot survive. It will suffer losses from theft of assets, credit card fraud, and record-keeping errors. The financial data it generates will be incorrect and unreliable, creating financial, legal, and regulatory problems. The company will enter into unauthorized transactions. It will suffer from operational inefficiencies and the failure to follow prescribed managerial policies. The quality of its products or services and the efficiency of its employees will decline.

Problem: Costs Not Closely Tracked

SYMPTOMS

- Critical documentation regarding costs to date does not exist or cannot be generated within the time required by financial management.

- Expenses are above or below budget amounts.

- Checks are missing.

- Many expenses are charged to cash or to miscellaneous expense and not to their proper accounts.

- Unusual or infrequent expenses are not recorded or recorded incorrectly.

- The chart of accounts appears to have been changed frequently to meet new reporting standards.

- Inventory and other assets are either overstated or understated.

- The ratio of gross profit to revenue is incorrect.

- Financial statements contain unreasonable expenditures or material omissions.

- Unauthorized individuals have access to blank checks and a check-writing machine and are forging checks for illegal and unauthorized payments.

- An audit by independent auditors discovers fraud and embezzlement by individual employees.

- The company issues unnumbered checks that are not recorded in the accounting records.

CAUSES

- There is an improper accounting policy regarding the documentation and recording of expenses.
- Management is inexperienced or incompetent.
- Internal control procedures are inadequate.
- A single individual controls disbursements.
- Payments are made without authorization from a higher level of authority.
- Internal controls applicable to the recording or disbursement of cash are inadequate or nonexistent.

MEASUREMENT AND ANALYSIS.   Except for extraordinary items, companies have considerable leeway in classifying expenses. Generally accepted accounting principles (GAAP) require that all items of profit and loss be recognized in the accounting period in which they occur. Expenses include accrual of estimated losses from loss contingencies, and are subject to budgetary controls, which can be very effective in highlighting deviations that require investigation. All expense items must be carefully recorded if net income is to be the effective criterion for measuring the performance of a company and estimating its future performance.

REPAIR

- Review and evaluate internal control procedures associated with recording expenses.
- Examine expense balances.
- Analyze large unexplained variations from budgeted or prior-year amounts in expense accounts.
- Review all accounting procedures, operations, and ratio tests.
- Investigate substantial deviations from budgeted amounts.
- Number all authorizations for payments and checks.
- Evaluate the accounting staff and retrain if necessary.
- Define the lines of responsibility for recording expenses and disbursing cash.
- Review all liability transactions to ensure that all expenses have been recorded for the accounting period.

PREVENTION TECHNIQUES

- Establish internal control procedures to record expenses.
- Design documentation to record and substantiate all cash disbursement transactions.
- Set up a chart of accounts for each asset, liability, capital, income, and expense account.
- Ensure that the accounting staff is honest, competent, and trustworthy.
- Ensure that the check-writing machine is used only by authorized personnel.
- Require cosigners for large checks.

SPILLOVER EFFECTS

- Incorrect financial decisions
- Audits
- Review by governmental agencies
- Lawsuits for mismanagement and negligence
- Declining prices for the company's stocks and bonds
- A downgraded credit rating
- Difficulty obtaining financing

See also CHECK FRAUD AND IMPROPER PAYMENTS, DISTORTED COST INFORMATION, INADEQUATE COST CONTROLS, CUMBERSOME ACCOUNTING PROCEDURES, and RECORDKEEPING ERRORS.

Problem: Assets Not Monitored

IDENTIFYING SYMPTOMS

- The company owns assets that are not recorded on the books or in the records or that cannot be located.
- Physical assets, such as plant and equipment, are obsolete, damaged, or have no value.
- The incidence of accounting errors related to the classification of all assets is abnormally high.
- The financial statement figures regarding assets are incorrect.
- Cash, inventory, and other assets are being stolen.
- The allowance for doubtful accounts is wrong, resulting in an unrealistic, unrealized accounts-receivable balance.

- Inaccurate depreciation and amortization methods have been applied to long-term assets.
- Goodwill, an intangible asset, is recorded on the books but in fact there is no reasonable basis for it.

CAUSES

- Lack of physical safeguards and internal control over both current and long-lived assets
- Technological innovations that make older assets, such as machinery and equipment, obsolete
- Inaccurate accounting records
- Failure to record asset purchases
- Theft by dishonest employees and outsiders
- Failure to keep valuable assets, such as securities, in a safe

The failure to record and classify assets and expenses may be due to an incompetent accounting staff, lack of internal controls, the failure to keep up-to-date records, and/or the use of incorrect accounting principles.

MEASUREMENT AND ANALYSIS. Business assets are separated into current assets and noncurrent assets with a useful life of more than one year. Current assets (including cash, short-term investments, accounts receivable, and inventory) tend to be more liquid than fixed assets and are more prone to theft than noncurrent assets. The cost of long-lived assets (consisting of long-term investments, land, buildings, and equipment, intangible assets, such as patents and copyrights, and minerals in the ground) includes their purchase price, transportation charges, brokerage commissions, legal fees, and back property taxes. Correct methods of depreciation, amortization, and depletion must be applied to these long-term assets.

REPAIR

- Review the chart of accounts that classifies transactions into balance sheet and income statement accounts.
- Evaluate all internal control procedures.
- Conduct training programs on the treatment of asset acquisitions.
- Where possible, put assets under lock and key.
- Investigate missing assets and file insurance claims to recover their cost.

- Examine vendors' invoices and related documents to verify acquisition of equipment.
- If goodwill appears on the books, determine how it was calculated.

PREVENTION TECHNIQUES

- Implement in-house training programs to ensure that the accounting staff is honest, competent, and trustworthy.
- Ensure that there are adequate documentation records and authorization for specific individual transactions.
- Safeguard physical assets and records. (For example, each physical asset should be given a serial number.)
- Establish independent checks on the accounting functions by both internal and external auditors.
- Inspect all assets purchased and received by the company.
- Record the cost of assets constructed.
- Hold the employee in charge of specific assets responsible for shortages or other discrepancies.
- Change locks and security codes periodically.

SPILLOVER EFFECTS.   If an accounting system and the accompanying internal control procedures are inadequate or inefficient, it will not generate reliable accounting information pertaining to assets. As a result, there will be misstatements regarding the financial position and operating results of the company. This will lead to incorrect financial decisions, audits, a decline in stock prices, reluctance by creditors to extend credit, and stockholder lawsuits.

See also RECORDKEEPING ERRORS, CUMBERSOME ACCOUNTING PROCEDURES, THEFT, MISCOUNTED INVENTORY, INACCURATE INVENTORY RECORDS, and COSTS NOT CLOSELY TRACKED.

Problem: Recordkeeping Errors

IDENTIFYING SYMPTOMS

- Misstated financial statement figures
- Restatement of previously prepared financial statements
- Extension of the audit report due date
- Incomplete records
- Duplication of effort

- Unproductive recordkeeping time
- The disclosure of employee fraud and embezzlement
- An increase in audit fees
- A constant turnover of outside auditors because of disagreements

CAUSES

- An incompetent or inexperienced accounting staff
- Lack of internal controls
- Absence of internal and external audits
- Deficient organizational structure
- Failure to define responsibility among employees
- Lack of up-to-date records
- The use of incorrect accounting principles

MEASUREMENT AND ANALYSIS

- Analyze the effect of recordkeeping errors on the financial statements.
- Determine the dollar amount of any theft and embezzlement.
- Evaluate the failure to meet deadlines in accumulating and reporting financial information.
- Determine the ratio of audit fees to sales. A high ratio indicates that more audit time was required because of problems with the company's accounting records or internal control procedures.

REPAIR

- Undertake internal and external audits to confirm financial statement figures.
- Prepare a monthly bank reconciliation to prove that the balance per books reconciles with the balance per bank.
- Count major assets, such as inventory and long-term assets, on a periodic basis.
- Correct errors immediately.
- Ask an independent CPA firm to evaluate the accounting system and make written recommendations for improvement.
- Use computerized accounting software packages to improve accuracy and timeliness.

- Establish individual packages for accounts receivable, accounts payable, cash receipts, cash payments, and other essential accounting functions.
- Make use of audit and tax preparation software programs.

PREVENTION TECHNIQUES

- Ensure that the accounting staff is honest, competent, and trustworthy.
- Separate duties to ensure proper internal control.
- Be sure that procedures are properly authorized and that documentation and records are adequate.
- Safeguard physical assets and records.
- Establish an independent check on the accounting functions by both internal and external auditors.
- Set up an audit committee to review all audit procedures.

SPILLOVER EFFECTS

- Lack of reliable accounting information
- Stockholder lawsuits
- A drop in the market value of equity shares
- Excessive loan restrictions
- Disallowance of certain expenditures by the Internal Revenue Service
- Incorrect financial management decisions
- Increased borrowing costs
- Decline in the value of the company's shares
- Difficulty issuing credit instruments

See also CUMBERSOME ACCOUNTING PROCEDURES and CHECK FRAUD AND IMPROPER PAYMENTS.

Problem: Credit Card Fraud

IDENTIFYING SYMPTOM. The unauthorized use of stolen or lost credit cards.

CAUSES

- Failure by employees to verify that the holder of the card is authorized to use it

- Failure of a bank to cancel a card when there has been a report of fraudulent charges on it
- Outdated information regarding lost or stolen credit cards.
- Employee fraud

MEASUREMENT AND ANALYSIS.   Credit cards offer consumers the convenience of buying goods without having to pay cash immediately. Retailers benefit because they do not have to check a customer's credit rating. However, credit card fraud is an inherent part of doing business. Millions of credit cards are in circulation today. A small percentage of them are lost or stolen annually, resulting in their unauthorized use by unscrupulous individuals.

REPAIR

- Train employees to verify that the person who presents the card for payment of a purchase is its true owner and is authorized to use it.
- Allow only specific employees to handle credit card purchases.

PREVENTION TECHNIQUES

- Check all credit card numbers for lost or stolen cards.
- Check the card's expiration date and the signature of the authorized user.
- Ask that the user show additional identification.
- Bond all employees who handle credit card transactions.
- Keep a file on all known customers who participate in fraudulent transactions involving credit cards.

SPILLOVER EFFECTS.   In the process of installing procedures to guard against credit card fraud, financial management should also evaluate the company's contract for credit card processing services. Because of competition in the industry, prices for these services have dropped sharply and improved options have proliferated.

Problem: Cumbersome Accounting Procedures

IDENTIFYING SYMPTOMS

- Outdatedness
- Net losses

- Abnormally high incidence of errors
- Misstated financial statement figures
- Restatement of previously prepared financial statements
- Extension of the audit report due date
- The generation of excess unimportant information
- Incomplete records
- Failure to disclose information
- Duplication of effort
- Unproductive time
- Theft of cash, inventory, and other assets
- Disclosure of employee fraud and embezzlement
- An expensive but necessary increase in amount of time outside auditors spend going over accounts
- Constant turnover in outside auditors because of disagreements

CAUSES

- Incompetent or inexperienced accounting staff
- Lack of internal controls
- Absence of internal and external audits
- Deficient organizational structure
- Failure to keep up-to-date records
- Use of incorrect accounting principles

MEASUREMENT AND ANALYSIS

- Analyze recordkeeping errors and their effect on the financial statements.
- Determine the dollar amount of the theft and embezzlement sustained.
- Analyze the reasons for the failure to meet deadlines in accumulating and reporting financial information.
- Evaluate the ratio of audit fees to sales. A high ratio indicates that more audit time was required because of problems with the company's accounting records.

REPAIR

- Ensure that internal controls are sufficient to safeguard assets.
- Immediately correct any accounting errors discovered.

PREVENTION TECHNIQUES

- Implement in-house training programs to assure that the accounting staff is up-to-date on the latest pronouncements of the American Institute of CPAs, the Financial Accounting Standards Board, and the Internal Revenue Service.

- Document transactions.

SPILLOVER EFFECTS.   If an accounting system is inadequate, it will not generate reliable information. As a result, misstatements may exist in financial position and operating results. This will lead to audits and disallowances by various governmental agencies. Creditors may also sue. Stringent loan restrictions will occur. There may be stockholder derivative suits.

See also RECORDKEEPING ERRORS.

13

Business Ownership Threatened

If a company cannot meet its impending obligations, it will become insolvent and possibly go bankrupt. Indications of looming problems include operating losses, cash deficiencies, failure to obtain credit, a sudden drop in the prices of a firm's securities, and a lack of cash realization in assets. Management can take many steps to protect itself against business failure, including avoiding excessive debt, staggering the company's debt payments, lengthening the maturity dates of debt, matching the maturity dates of debt with the maturity dates of assets (hedging), selling off unprofitable business segments and low return assets, obtaining adequate insurance, diversifying horizontally and vertically, avoiding markets on the downturn or those that are highly competitive, and not overextending itself either financially or operationally.

Another threat is hostile takeover by another firm. If this occurs, the takeover may lead to increased costs, lack of financial synergies, and employee resentment.

Problem: Bankruptcy Looms

IDENTIFYING SYMPTOMS

- Declining profitability or increasing losses
- Cash flow inadequacies
- Inability to pay liabilities on their due dates
- Unavailability of financing
- The outside auditor's withdrawal from the engagement
- Contraction in the business
- Cessation of dividends
- Violation of loan agreements
- Lawsuits
- Criminal and civil charges

- Sharp decline in credit rating
- Significant decline in the price of stocks and bonds
- Increased business risk

CAUSES

- Deficient financial health
- Poor financial planning and management
- Lack of financial goals and objectives
- Lawsuits
- Product line deficiencies
- Unethical conduct
- Poor relationship with creditors and investors
- Inadequate insurance against losses
- Lack of cash
- Use of too much leverage
- Inability to raise money due to poor credit rating
- Incompetent professional management
- Damages and legal costs paid in litigation; criminal as well as civil penalties may be involved, and the reputation of the business may be ruined (as in the case of product liability)

MEASUREMENT AND ANALYSIS. In a study done by W. Beaver[1] it was found that bankruptcy could be predicted at least five years prior to such occurrence by looking at certain key ratios—the most important being cash flow to total debt, net income to total assets, and total debt to total assets. W. Beaver's cash flow ratio (net income plus depreciation divided by total debt) predicts bankruptcy within the next two years if the ratio is less than 1.

E. Altman[2] formulated a mathematical model, termed the "Z-score," that is useful in predicting bankruptcy within the short run (one or two years). The "Z-score" equals:

[1] W. Beaver, "Financial Ratios as Predictors of Failure," *Empirical Research in Accounting: Selected Studies, (1966),* Supplement to Volume 4, *Journal of Accounting Research,* pp. 77–111.

[2] E. Altman, "Financial Ratios, Discriminant Analysis and the Prediction of Corporate Bankruptcy," *The Journal of Finance,* (September 1978), pp. 589–609.

$$\frac{\text{Working capital}}{\text{Total assets}} \times 1.2 + \frac{\text{retained earnings}}{\text{total assets}} \times 1.4$$

$$+ \frac{\text{operating income}}{\text{total assets}} \times 3.3$$

$$+ \frac{\text{market value of common stock and preferred stock (or net worth for private companies)}}{\text{total debt}} \times .6$$

$$+ \frac{\text{sales}}{\text{total assets}} \times 1$$

Altman's scoring chart follows:

Score	Probability of short-term illiquidity
1.80 or less	Very high
1.81 to 2.7	High
2.8 to 2.9	Possible
3.0 or higher	Not likely

The score is important to management in indicating whether capital expansion and dividends should be curtailed to keep needed funds within the business.

Example: Company H provides the following relevant data.

Working capital	$250,000
Total assets	900,000
Total liabilities	300,000
Retained earnings	200,000
Sales	1,000,000
Operating income	150,000
Common stock	
Book value	210,000
Market value	300,000
Preferred stock	
Book value	100,000
Market value	160,000

The "Z-score" is:

$$\frac{\$250,000}{\$900,000} \times 1.2 + \frac{\$200,000}{\$900,000} \times 1.4 + \frac{\$150,000}{\$900,000} \times 3.3 + \frac{\$460,000}{\$300,000} \times .6$$

$$+ \frac{\$1,000,000}{\$900,000} \times 1 = .333 + .311 + .550 + .920 + 1.111 = \underline{3.225}$$

The score indicates that the probability of failure is unlikely.

E. Altman, R. Haldeman, and P. Narayanan[3] uncovered the following measures as best for forecasting bankruptcy: operating income to total assets, earnings stability, times-interest-earned, retained earnings to total assets, current ratio, common equity to total capital, and total assets.

For a fee, ZETA Services will determine the possibility of business failure within 5 years through the use of their "secret" ZETA model.

REPAIR

- Lengthen the maturity dates of debt and modify interest rates.
- Sell off unprofitable business segments and low-return assets.
- Restrict capital expansion during economic downturns.
- Reduce prices on slow-moving inventory.

PREVENTION TECHNIQUES

- Avoid excessive debt and stagger debt payments.
- Anticipate future trends in the marketplace.
- Assure the adequacy of insurance coverage.
- Be careful about going from a labor-intensive to a capital-intensive one when the economy looks dismal.
- Make required expenditures for future growth, such as research and development.
- Avoid operations in risky areas.
- Emphasize the hedging approach to finance by matching the due dates on debt to the maturity dates of assets.
- Keep up-to-date with changes in technology.
- Diversify horizontally and vertically.
- Avoid moving into industries with a history of failure.
- Avoid long-term, fixed-fee contracts.
- Avoid markets on the downturn or those that are very competitive.
- Do not overextend financially or operationally.
- Manage assets, such as cash, receivables, and inventory, to receive attractive returns while controlling risk.

---

[3]E. Altman, R. Haldeman, and P. Narayanan, "ZETA Analysis: A New Model to Identify Bankruptcy Risk of Corporations," *Journal of Banking and Finance* (1977), pp. 29–54.

SPILLOVER EFFECTS

- Lawsuits for damages caused to creditors and investors because of poor financial management
- Loss of jobs by financial managers and other employees
- Legal costs and other administrative expenses incurred in the process of liquidating or reorganizing the company

See also EXCESSIVE DEBT, INADEQUATE LIQUIDITY, and INSOLVENCY.

Problem: Inability to Curb Financial Problems

IDENTIFYING SYMPTOMS

- A company makes radical policy changes too quickly.
- Decisions are based on intuition rather than on detailed research about market conditions.
- Critical daily problems are not resolved.
- The company has not had a significant product or service success in years and is considered a follower rather than a leader in its industry.
- The company is not keeping up with market, technological, and industry trends.
- The firm continues to lose money after developing products and fails to establish a foothold in the market.
- Targeted production goals and quotas are not met, are late, and/or are over budget.
- While diversifying to reduce risk, the organization is doing nothing for its shareholders.
- Creditors are not being paid.
- There are union grievances by employees claiming unfair treatment.
- There is a high degree of employee turnover.
- Customers complain about the poor quality of the company's services and products.
- There is an excessive return of the company's products and recalls for faulty manufacture or design.
- The company is experiencing negative publicity.
- The firm is marginally profitable and suffers from cash flow problems and declining sales.

- Dividends are paid from borrowed funds.
- There are erroneous and fraudulent financial statements and the waste and theft of assets.
- The annual report is delayed.
- Questionable accounting practices are in use.
- Executive management is taking excessive compensation payments and fringe benefits during a period of low earning power.

CAUSES

- Failure to develop new products
- Failure to preserve basic major historical markets
- Deterioration in operational efficiency
- Unproductive diversification
- Poor-quality products
- Questionable financial policies
- Resources diverted to new ventures where management lacks expertise
- Unstable management due to high turnover
- Lack of experience on the part of management
- Lack of cooperation between management and labor
- Lack of ethics and ideals
- Poor example set by upper management
- Workers pressed for concessions, without similar actions on the part of management
- Variable costs exceeding variable revenue
- Highly technical products that break down frequently

MEASUREMENT AND ANALYSIS

- Examine the trend in company units produced relative to industry units produced, and analyze company revenue as a percent of total industry revenue.
- Examine the trend in profit margin, operating expenses to revenue, manufacturing cost to revenue, and inventory turnover.
- Examine the extent to which cost changes relative to changes in sales.
- Compare company costs relative to those of other companies in the industry.

REPAIR

- Improve operational effectiveness.
- Develop highly differentiated products at low cost.
- Retire or terminate unproductive employees.
- Put financial management personnel in control of expenditures.
- Conduct studies to determine what customers are buying.
- Ensure that the company develops a reputation for integrity and fairness.
- Focus on fewer products of higher quality.
- Restructure, to divest the firm of marginal or nonprofitable branches, divisions, and subsidiaries.
- Eliminate excesses in parts of the organization.
- Use as a rule of thumb: four top level officers per $1 billion in sales.
- Form committees to study each of the company's problem areas. A compensation committee could be formed to review the benefits package given to key employees, for example, while a sales committee could be formed to evaluate the company's advertising program.
- Retain earnings and establish new lines of credit.
- Review the dividend policy of the company. The dividend payments may be too high relative to the company's limited profit picture.
- Consider selling common stock to generate funds for the acquisition of a limited number of companies with a proven earnings record. (This policy carries the caveat that too much diversification may put the company back into financial instability.)
- Restrict dividend payments.
- Redesign products to lower manufacturing costs.
- Institute a review of production facilities and replace or retool machinery that has a record of malfunctioning in production.

PREVENTION TECHNIQUES

- Send experienced financial trouble-shooting teams to different divisions, departments, and subsidiaries to solve problems.
- Clearly state the company's policies and production goals.
- Make financial decisions after all information has been accumulated from several independent sources to confirm its accuracy.
- Protect established markets before attempting to develop new ones.

- Become a low-cost provider of distinguished products and services.
- Standardize production parts.
- Invest in facilities that produce only profitable items that are in demand.
- Improve the technical abilities of current financial management.
- Offer early retirement to older, less competent managers. Hire people with a proven record of success.
- Attempt to renegotiate prices with suppliers or seek cheaper alternate sources of supply.

SPILLOVER EFFECTS.   If financial management is unable to alter the operating policy of the company, it may fail and seek bankruptcy or reorganization protection.

See also BANKRUPTCY LOOMS, INADEQUATE LIQUIDITY, and INSOLVENCY. For an informative, complete discussion of this topic, see Frederick Zimmerman, *The Turnaround Experience: Real World Lessons in Revitalizing Corporations* (New York: McGraw-Hill, 1991).

Problem: Inability to Repay Debt

IDENTIFYING SYMPTOMS

- The business is short on cash inflows.
- The company has difficulty obtaining financing.
- The firm has difficulty collecting notes and accounts receivable, converting short-term investments into cash, and obtaining credit from suppliers.
- The company cannot buy inventory or assets, has low profitability, and cannot take cash discounts by making early payment.
- The organization's credit rating is deteriorating.
- Fixed interest costs are high, and debt is excessive.

CAUSES

- Inability to obtain funds to finance expansion
- Poor operating performance, coupled with deficient cash flow
- Liabilities in excess of the company's ability to pay
- Additional debt incurred in an attempt to prevent a hostile takeover by another company
- Management incompetence

MEASUREMENT AND ANALYSIS. There are many measures to appraise a company's ability to repay debt. *See* INADEQUATE LIQUIDITY and INSOLVENCY in Chapter 5 for full coverage of them.

REPAIR

- Reduce company expansion or obtain additional financing.
- Sell assets.
- Change the amount and timing of future cash flows in order to adjust to sudden developments.
- Offer creditors stock in place of cash repayment of debt.

PREVENTION TECHNIQUES

- Better planning for the acquisition of capital facilities
- Reducing expansion efforts
- Securing new lines of credit
- Synchronizing cash outlays to cash inflows
- Improving the budgeting process to forecast the demand for capital expenditures so that funds are available to repay debt
- Improved financial planning to anticipate future conditions in the economy and money market
- Using the hedging approach to financing by matching the maturity dates of debt to the collection date or maturity date of all assets

SPILLOVER EFFECTS. A poor working capital position means that the company is less liquid. Inadequate liquidity will result in lower credit ratings, decline in the market price of the issuing company's stocks and bonds, higher interest rates to borrow, unavailability of financing, financial inability to make profitable investments at the right time, and, in severe cases, insolvency and bankruptcy.

If debts cannot be repaid, there will be an increased cost of capital, higher compensating balances, increased business risk, higher financing costs, and financial instability. A business may fail if it cannot obtain credit to meet its contractual financial obligations.

A company that is out of cash cannot operate effectively and its profitability will decline.

See also INADEQUATE LIQUIDITY, INABILITY TO OBTAIN FINANCING, BANKRUPTCY LOOMS, EXCESSIVE DEBT, INADEQUATE WORKING CAPITAL, INSOLVENCY, POOR PROFITABILITY AND GROWTH, INADEQUATE CASH POSITION, and CASH OUTFLOWS EXCEED CASH INFLOWS.

Problem: Takeover Threat

IDENTIFYING SYMPTOMS

- The market value of the company's common stock is below its book value.

- The company has incurred continuous operating losses and has a tax-loss carryforward that makes it an attractive takeover candidate.

- The company is cash-rich and has significant growth potential or a low debt/equity ratio.

CAUSES. A purchaser, or raider, seeks to acquire another company for several reasons:

- The target company may own highly liquid assets, have a high rate of return, own one or more successful products, have successful management and sales teams, have developed a reputation for reliability and integrity, offer research capability, and/or have established profitable sales territories that the acquiring company seeks to penetrate.

- The purchaser may be seeking to eliminate competition by acquiring a competitor.

- The purchaser wants to diversify its operations.

- The purchaser may also be pursuing a policy of external growth over internal growth. External growth might be the best solution for the purchaser if the target company has low cost assets, greater economy of scale, a better and more secure supply of raw materials, a reliable source of labor and managerial skills, the possibility for rapid growth, and the opportunity to diversify the purchaser's product line.

- The purchaser may be seeking to offset the operating loss of the target company against its own profits, thereby achieving considerable tax savings.

- The raider is trying to smooth out the cyclical movement of its earnings.

MEASUREMENT AND ANALYSIS. The term *business combination* refers to any situation in which two or more organizations are joined together in common ownership. Business combinations can be accomplished in various ways. First, a company can acquire the *assets, and possibly the liabilities,* of the target company in exchange for cash and stock. In an alternative approach, a company can acquire the stock of the target company in exchange for cash and stock. In yet another gambit, a company can achieve legal control over another company simply by acquiring a majority of the voting stock of the target company.

After a takeover, the acquiring company has control of the target company and may either retain the acquired company as a separate legal entity or dissolve it. If the acquired company continues to function, it must maintain its own corporate officers, board of directors, and independent accounting system. The acquiring company, or purchaser, may elect to file consolidated tax returns if it makes certain tax elections available under the Internal Revenue Code. This enables both the purchaser and target company to offset any operating losses generated by one company against the profits of the other.

REPAIR. Current business strategy places emphasis on the continuous expansion of major corporate organizations. To avoid an unfriendly takeover by a raider, management might turn to one or more of the antitakeover measures called "shark repellents":

- *Rescue by a "white knight."* In this move, the target company is "saved" by a third, "friendly" company that is willing to enter into a bidding war against the first purchaser.

- *Use of the "Pacman" defense.* In this countermove, the target company makes a takeover bid of its own for the stock of the company attempting to take it over.

- *Use of a "poison pill."* In this tactic, the target company makes its acquisition more expensive for the raider by enacting a provision (the "poison pill") whereby its current shareholders can purchase additional shares at a price well below market value.

- *Use of "greenmail."* In what is essentially an effort to "buy off" the raider, the target of the takeover enters into a transaction whereby it pays the raider a premium ("greenmail") well over the shares' market price.

PREVENTION TECHNIQUES

- Stagger the terms of the board of directors over several years, so that the entire board of directors does not come up for election all at once. A potential raider will thus have difficulty electing its own board of directors to gain control.

- Amend the corporate charter to require that a supermajority of voting shares be required to approve any takeover proposals.

- Sue to delay a takeover and to make it more expensive and less attractive to the raider.

SPILLOVER EFFECTS. The acquisition of another company in the same industry may trigger antitrust action. If the takeover bid is successful, the purchaser may also have to decide whether the acquisition is to be treated and accounted for as a "pooling of interests" or a "purchase." An unsuccessful takeover may have a negative effect on earnings, due to inefficiencies in the combined unit.

See also COSTS INCREASE AFTER ACQUISITION and FINANCIAL INCONSISTENCIES AFTER ACQUISITION.

Problem: Costs Increase After Acquisition

IDENTIFYING SYMPTOMS

- Operating costs increase disproportionately in relation to combined revenues.
- The expected synergistic effect on earnings does not materialize.
- Both companies' earnings per share decrease.

CAUSES

- The acquisition of incompatible or obsolete assets
- Duplicate production facilities
- Adjustment of pay scales
- Too many nonproductive employees
- Costs of servicing acquisition debt
- Higher insurance costs because of increased risks
- Legal and accounting costs
- Unsuccessful defense strategies that result in substantial residual costs
- An outflow of valuable managerial talent

MEASUREMENT AND ANALYSIS.

A variety of preacquisition expenses may be incurred in consummating a corporate takeover: the organizational costs of a subsidiary created to acquire the target corporation, the start-up expenses of the newly created subsidiary corporation, the takeover defense expenses of the target corporation, and the greenmail expenses of either the purchaser or target corporation.

REPAIR

- After the acquisition, announce what the policy of the new management will be. This procedure will reduce employee anxieties and public rumors that may be adversely affecting the market value of the purchaser's shares.

- Formulate consistent accounting procedures for both companies, so that reporting results are not inconsistent.
- Adopt similar tax policies.
- Writeoff obsolete inventory
- Sell off or close duplicate production facilities and use the proceeds to retire outstanding debt.
- Terminate nonproductive and nonessential employees.
- Use the operating loss of the target company to reduce the purchaser's taxes.
- Examine the dividend policy of both companies. A continuity of dividend payments for both companies can reassure investors.
- Treat the acquisition as a pooling of interests. (Poolings require virtually no cash or new debt to complete.)

PREVENTION TECHNIQUES

- Adopt a uniform accounting policy for both companies to avoid inconsistent and misleading financial statements.
- Prepare consolidated financial statements to diminish the firm's overall risk and increase the price/earnings (P/E) ratio even if potential earnings growth is unchanged.

SPILLOVER EFFECTS

- Labor problems
- Negative publicity
- A reduction in the market value of the purchaser's outstanding shares
- The payout of "golden parachutes" (termination payments to discharged executives)
- Legal costs

See also COSTS INCREASE AFTER ACQUISITION, FINANCIAL INCONSISTENCIES AFTER ACQUISITION, and TAKEOVER THREAT.

Problem: Financial Inconsistencies After Acquisition

IDENTIFYING SYMPTOMS

- Financial statements are composed of inconsistent accounting principles, policies, unrealistic accounting estimates, and differences in the tax treatment of major transactions.

- The calendar year-end for each company is different.
- Operating costs bear no relationship to revenues. The expected synergistic effect from the acquisition of another company does not materialize.

CAUSE.   Inconsistent accounting treatment for revenue and expenses.

MEASUREMENT AND ANALYSIS

- Analyze the accounting policies of both companies and their effect on their financial statements.
- Study any cash flow problems.

REPAIR

- Make all accounting procedures consistent.
- Retrain the accounting staff.

PREVENTION TECHNIQUES

- Form an accounting committee to evaluate the advantages of changes in the method of accounting.
- Ensure that the accounting staff is current on the latest pronouncements of the American Institute of CPAs, the Financial Accounting Standards Board, and the Internal Revenue Service.

SPILLOVER EFFECT.   A financial picture that is misleading to creditors and investors.

See also COSTS INCREASE AFTER ACQUISITION, TAKEOVER THREAT, MANAGEMENT UNAWARE OF FINANCIAL PROBLEMS, and CUMBERSOME ACCOUNTING PROCEDURES.

14

Tax Planning and Preparation

Tax avoidance is merely tax minimization using legal and accounting techniques. In this sense, it becomes the proper objective of all tax planning. Inadequate or improper tax recordkeeping can result in misstated tax return data, placing the business in possible civil and criminal violation of the Internal Revenue Code. Underpayment of taxes can result in penalties, as well as in civil and/or criminal liability, depending upon its nature. Improper tax planning will usually cause a higher than normal tax burden and lower profits. All tax-planning strategies must be fully recognized and utilized when appropriate.

Problem: Sloppy Tax Recordkeeping

IDENTIFYING SYMPTOMS

- An abnormally high incidence of errors affecting the company's tax liability
- Misstated financial statement figures
- Lack of tax documentation
- Ignorance of tax laws
- Failure to define staff responsibilities relating to the filing of tax reports
- Stockholder lawsuits charging that opportunities for large tax savings were lost
- The imposition of additional taxes, interest, and penalties by the Internal Revenue Service and various state tax departments
- Excessive payments of professional fees to tax accountants and lawyers

CAUSES

- An incompetent or inexperienced accounting staff
- Lack of internal controls
- Deficient organizational structure relating to tax reporting

- Failure by management to keep current with changes in the tax laws
- Use of incorrect tax-accounting principles

MEASUREMENT AND ANALYSIS

- Review the accuracy and appropriateness of tax recordkeeping.
- Analyze the errors that have occurred and their effect on the firm's financial statements.
- Evaluate the reasons for the company's inability to meet tax filing deadlines and its failure to make favorable tax elections.

REPAIR

- Define staff responsibility for tax accounting and filings.
- Ask the independent CPA firm to evaluate tax preparation software programs.
- Analyze the effect of terms and conditions imposed on the company by the Internal Revenue Service.
- Hire competent tax accountants.

PREVENTION TECHNIQUE.   Ensure that the accounting staff is current on tax law and procedures.

SPILLOVER EFFECTS

- Excessive nondeductible tax penalties and high interest charges
- Charges of inept and negligent management as well as excessive corporate waste
- Audits by the Internal Revenue Service
- Stockholder derivative suits

See also RECORDKEEPING ERRORS, LACK OF COST INFORMATION, UNDERPAYMENT OF TAXES, and CUMBERSOME ACCOUNTING PROCEDURES.

Problem: Underpayment of Taxes

IDENTIFYING SYMPTOMS

- Penalty statements from the Internal Revenue Service and state tax departments

- Warnings from the internal audit staff, outside independent auditors, and/or legal counsel that the enterprise is not making its quarterly estimated payments

CAUSES

- Failure to define staff responsibilities
- Ignorance of tax laws
- Weak internal control
- Lack of operating cash

MEASUREMENT AND ANALYSIS.   To figure the correct estimated corporate tax, the enterprise must calculate its expected sales, other income (such as dividend and interest received from outside investments), expenses, taxable income, estimated tax liability, and available tax credits.

REPAIR

- Define staff responsibility for making estimated tax payments.
- Announce the due dates of all estimated tax payments.

PREVENTION TECHNIQUES

- Train the accounting staff to recognize tax problems that affect the firm's tax liability.
- Prepare a quarterly income statement calculating the amount of the quarterly estimated tax payment.

SPILLOVER EFFECTS

- Excessive nondeductible tax penalties and high interest charges
- Charges of inept and negligent management

Problem: Double Taxation

IDENTIFYING SYMPTOM.   The corporation is paying a tax at a rate of 15 percent to 34 percent, leaving less available to the shareholders in the form of a distributable dividend. Any amount subsequently distributed as a dividend to shareholders is again subject to taxation at the individual level.

CAUSE.   Failure to elect S corporation status.

MEASUREMENT AND ANALYSIS.   To avoid double taxation, elect S corporation status. To make the election, three shareholder requirements must be satisfied on each day of the tax year:

1. The corporation may not have more than 35 shareholders.
2. All shareholders must be individuals, estates, or certain kinds of trusts.
3. The shareholders cannot be nonresident aliens.

The corporation's election of S corporation status is valid only if all shareholders consent to the election. The election to be treated as an S corporation can be made at any time during the entire tax year before the election year, or on or before the 15th day of the third month of the election year. Form 2553 must be used. The corporation must have authorized and issued only one class of either voting or nonvoting common stock. Every S corporation must then file a return on Form 1120S for each subsequent tax year.

The S corporation rules were enacted to permit small corporations to enjoy the nontax advantages of corporations without being subject to double taxation. Upon election as an S corporation, the tax treatment is almost like that of partnership taxation, in that the income and losses of the corporation flow through, under the conduit principle, directly to the shareholders.

REPAIR.   Elect S corporation status.

PREVENTION TECHNIQUES

- Comply with the applicable tax statutes for S corporations.
- Monitor all transfers of S corporation stock to make sure that the transferee is not an ineligible shareholder.
- Establish procedures for purchasing the stock of deceased shareholders.
- Make sure, when selling stock, that the number of shareholders does not exceed 35.
- Supervise all S corporation investment activities to ensure that passive investment income limitations for S corporations are not violated. (*Passive investment income* generally means gross receipts from interest, dividends, rents, royalties, annuities, and gains from sales or exchanges of stock or securities.) If an S corporation has passive income in excess of 25 percent of its gross receipts for three consecutive years, the S election is terminated as of the beginning of the following tax year.

SPILLOVER EFFECTS.   The structure of an S corporation can create hardships to shareholders who receive large amounts of income flowing through without actual distributions of cash with which to help pay the tax on the income. The election of S corporation status also prevents a corporation from allowing the accumulation of profit in the corporation with the intent of declaring a dividend at a later date, when shareholders may be in a lower tax bracket. An S corporation cannot issue both common and preferred stock. This limitation on the capital structure of an S corporation status will also prevent the corporation from going public, unless it elects to revoke its S election.

Problem: Avoiding Tax on the Transfer of Property

IDENTIFYING SYMPTOM.   The taxpayer or taxpayers are operating as either a sole proprietorship or partnership and are fearful of unlimited personal liability for legal obligations or negligent actions committed within the scope of the business.

CAUSES

- The enterprise is growing, thereby forcing the owners to incur greater liabilities.
- A growing workforce and the possibility of product liability require that the owners protect themselves behind a corporate shield that permits limited liability.

MEASUREMENT AND ANALYSIS.   Section 351 Internal Revenue Code, which involves a tax-free exchange, can apply to transfers to an existing corporation as well as transfers to a newly created corporation. The nonrecognition of gain or loss reflects the principle of continuity of the taxpayer's original investment. There is no real change in the taxpayer's economic status. The reorganization must be done according to a plan adopted in advance and will not be tax-free unless the exchange comes within the scope of the plan. The investment in certain properties used in the operation of the sole proprietorship or partnership carries over to the investment in corporate stock.

REPAIR.   Form a tax-free incorporation. Control, pursuant to Section 351, requires the person or persons transferring the property (money and other kinds of property such as accounts receivable, inventory, and equipment) to own stock representing at least 80 percent of the total combined voting power of all classes of stock entitled to vote and at least 80 percent of the total number of shares of all other classes of stock of the corporation. Under the code, any type of stock of the controlled corporation, whether preferred or common, voting or nonvoting, may be received by the transferors. Section 351 is mandatory and not elective.

PREVENTION TECHNIQUES.   To ensure tax-free incorporation the party or parties must meet the code definition of control. To qualify as a nontaxable transaction under the Internal Revenue Code, the transferor or transferors must be in control of the corporation immediately after the exchange. If the transfer meets the requirements stated under Section 351, no gain or loss will be recognized to the transferors pursuant to the exchange plan.

SPILLOVER EFFECTS

- A lengthy period of time between transfers can cause tax problems if the IRS does not consider the transfers part of a single plan.
- If an individual performs services for the corporation in return for stock, he or she will be taxed on the value of the stock issued for such services. Failure to follow the stringent requirements of the Internal Revenue Code may cause the recognition of a taxable gain on the transfer of property to the corporation. The recognition of a gain may be advantageous if the taxpayer is in a low tax bracket and not be subject to a high tax liability. In addition, a taxpayer who incurs a large capital gain may be able to offset the gain against substantial capital losses.

Problem: Incorrect Classification of Employees

IDENTIFYING SYMPTOMS

- Payroll costs are not being recorded.
- Tax agencies are constantly monitoring the employer's books and records to investigate possible payroll violations.
- Union representatives claim that the employer is not adhering to the union contract regarding payments of certain vacation and fringe benefits to employees.

CAUSES

- Management is treating the payroll expenditures as those applicable to an independent contractor (which would not require the payment of payroll taxes and other employee benefits). These unrecorded payroll costs result in erroneous product and expense costs.

- Company policy fails to differentiate between who is an independent contractor and who is an employee. (An independent contractor is an individual or firm who agrees to do a particular job for another.)

MEASUREMENT AND ANALYSIS.   The employment of an outside auditor, attorney, or contractor to perform a function specifically entailing the use of that person's professional skills is usually indicative of the services of an independent contractor. Internal Revenue Regulations provide that physicians, lawyers, contractors, "and others who follow an independent trade, business, or profession, in which they offer their services to the public, are not employees." This distinction incorporates the basic concept of what is an independent contractor.

Where the employer controls the quality of the performance, the hours of employment, and provides the tools necessary to complete the assigned task, the individual is properly classified as an employee and subject to payroll taxes, Social Security expenses, federal and state unemployment insurance, workers compensation, and union and pension benefits.

Under the Internal Revenue Code, an employer is liable for amounts required to be deducted and withheld from the wages of an employee. The code also contains numerous civil penalties, imposed for diverse but sometimes overlapping delinquencies, such as failure to file, negligence, and fraud.

REPAIR

- Study federal, state, and local laws for their definition of who is an employee and who may be properly classified as an independent contractor.

- Review old payroll audits to learn how management classified the individuals' employment status.

PREVENTION TECHNIQUES

- When hiring new employees, have them fill out a complete employment record, including their name, address, Social Security number, past employment history, and education and the company function for which they were hired.

- Have the internal audit staff and the outside independent accountants review all service contracts and employment forms to determine whether an individual is an independent contractor or an employee.

- Request a revenue ruling from the Internal Revenue Service if the status of a newly hired employee is unclear.
- Train accounting and personnel staff in the proper classification of newly hired employees.

SPILLOVER EFFECTS

- If the enterprise self-constructs its own assets, unrecorded payroll costs may lead to the undervaluation of inventory and depreciable assets.
- Interest and penalties may be levied for failure to pay appropriate payroll taxes.
- Stockholder lawsuits may ensue.
- Expensive additional payroll tax audits may be necessary to assist outside government and union auditors.

Problem: Fringe Benefits Not Recorded as Income

IDENTIFYING SYMPTOMS

- Penalty statements from the Internal Revenue Service and state tax departments
- Warnings that the enterprise is failing to report miscellaneous fringe benefits as taxable income
- Complaints from employees that they have been questioned by the Internal Revenue Service as to whether they have received certain taxable company benefits that have not been reported on their personal tax return

CAUSES

- Failure to define staff responsibilities
- Ignorance of tax laws
- Weak internal control
- Inexperienced staff

MEASUREMENT AND ANALYSIS.   When a fringe benefit is taxable, the amount includable in gross income generally equals the fair market value of the benefit, reduced by the amount, if any, paid by the employee for it. The cost to the employer is generally not relevant.

Certain fringe benefits are nontaxable if the employee receives services, not property, if the employer does not incur substantial cost, and if the services are offered to customers in the ordinary course of the business in which the employee works. These nontaxable employee benefits include:

- No-additional-cost services, such as allowing an airline employee to fly free
- Qualified employee discounts
- Working-condition fringe benefits, such as the free use of a company parking space
- *De minimus* fringe benefits, such as permitting a company secretary to type a personal letter

REPAIR

- Review company records to determine who has use of the company automobile, company-paid membership in country clubs, or who received tickets to entertainment events.
- Identify taxable and nontaxable employee benefits in writing.

PREVENTION TECHNIQUES

- Train accounting staff to recognize taxable benefits.
- Periodically review accounting records to determine which benefits, if any, are taxable.
- Have a stated policy for valuing taxable fringe benefits.

SPILLOVER EFFECTS

- Excessive nondeductible tax penalties and high interest charges
- Audits of the personal tax returns of employees who received taxable fringe benefits but did not report them

Problem: Excessive Compensation to Employee Shareholders

IDENTIFYING SYMPTOMS

- Salaries in excess of those ordinarily paid for similar services
- Excessive payments bear a close relationship to the stockholdings of officers

CAUSE.   The desire by management to distribute a dividend to employee-shareholders in the form of tax deductible salary payments.

MEASUREMENT AND ANALYSIS.   There may be included among the ordinary and necessary expenses paid or incurred in carrying on any trade or business a reasonable allowance for salaries and other compensation for personal services actually rendered to the corporation by an employee who is also a shareholder. The employee is usually a corporate officer. The test of deductibility in the case of compensation payments is whether they are in fact payment purely for services rendered to the corporation. If it is determined that the amount of compensation is in fact not payment for services rendered, it is not deductible by the corporation and will be treated by the Internal Revenue Service as the distribution of a dividend.

There is no precise rule to determine the exact amount of compensation that is considered reasonable. It may be assumed that reasonable and true compensation is only the amount that would ordinarily be paid for like services by similar enterprises under similar circumstances. The circumstances to be considered are those existing when the contract for services was made, not those existing when the contract is questioned by the Internal Revenue Service. The failure of a closely-held corporation to pay nondeductible dividends is a very significant factor in determining the allowable deduction for compensation paid to employee-shareholders. If the payments for compensation bear a close relationship to stockholdings and are found to be distributions of earnings or profits, the excessive payments will be treated as a nondeductible dividend.

The Internal Revenue Service can also examine a situation in which an employee-shareholder with a controlling interest in a corporation receives a large payment of compensation, especially in cases where the corporation has a history of paying small dividends.

REPAIR

- Upon examination by the Internal Revenue Service, the corporation must show that the compensation was ordinary and necessary and paid or incurred in carrying on the business

- The corporation must also show that the payments represent the purchase price for services rendered to the corporation and that the amount is fair and reasonable.

PREVENTION TECHNIQUES

- Prepare a checklist of factors that were used to determine the compensation for the employee, including:

  Employee's qualifications
  Number of available persons capable of performing the duties of the position

Nature and extent of the employee's work

Size and complexity of the business

Profitability of the corporation

Prevailing economic conditions

A comparison of salaries paid with dividend distributions to shareholders, and small corporations with a limited number of employee-shareholders

Amount of compensation paid to a particular employee in previous years

- The employee-shareholder can enter into "hedge-agreement" with the corporation stating that in case any portion of the salary paid is disallowed by the Internal Revenue Service the employee will refund the excess amount to the corporation, thereby permitting the enterprise to recoup excess funds.

SPILLOVER EFFECTS

- Continuous audits by the Internal Revenue Service
- Inclusion of excessive payments for salaries and other compensation for personal services in the gross income of the recipient

Problem: Funds Insufficient to Purchase a Deceased Shareholder's Stock

IDENTIFYING SYMPTOM. The corporation lacks the funds necessary to purchase a deceased shareholder's stock (as it is required by prior agreement to do, or as it simply wants to do so that the shares are not sold to strangers or vulnerable to purchase by a hostile shareholder group).

CAUSES

- A lack of cash
- Litigation preventing acquisition of stock

MEASUREMENT AND ANALYSIS. The most significant disadvantage of the shareholder stock repurchase plan is that the corporation may lack the necessary funds.

REPAIR. Use life insurance, purchased by and payable to the corporation, to fund the corporation's repurchase obligation upon the death of a shareholder.

PREVENTION TECHNIQUES. The parties will sometimes want to take the proceeds into account in determining the price to be paid by the corporation for the decedent's stock. This axiom is based on a principle of fairness. For example, if a corporation receives $100,000 as the result of a shareholder's death, and pays $10,000 for the book value of the stock, the remaining shareholders will share unexpended proceeds of $90,000 ($100,000 − $10,000). If, on the other hand, the increased value of the corporation is used in evaluating the purchase price of the decedent's stock, the decedent's estate will receive the fair market value of the stock without giving the remaining shareholders an unintended windfall.

Careful attention must be given when setting up insurance in connection with a death redemption agreement. The corporation should be the owner and beneficiary of the insurance policy. The proceeds should not be set at the minimum price to be paid for the decedent shareholder's stock.

SPILLOVER EFFECTS. The Internal Revenue Service may argue that the premiums paid by the corporation were taxable income to the insured shareholder because the shareholder is the real or beneficial owner of the insurance policy.

Glossary

Absorption (full) costing The cost of a product is the full unit manufacturing cost, consisting of direct materials, direct labor, and factory overhead.

Beta A measure of the company's risk relative to the market. It is the variation in the price of the company's stock relative to the variation in a stock market index (e.g., Standard and Poor's 500). A beta less than 1 means that the company's stock is less risky than the market.

Break-even point The sales volume in which total revenue equals total cost, resulting in a zero profit.

Capital Asset Pricing Model (CAPM) The model shows the relationship between an investment's expected (or required) return and its beta.

Capital gain (loss) The appreciation (depreciation) in market value.

Cash earnings Cash revenue less cash expenses. It is the net income backed up by cash flow from operations.

Compensating balance A deposit that a bank can use to offset an unpaid loan. No interest is earned on the compensating balance, which is stated as a percentage of the loan. It increases the effective interest rate on the loan.

Contribution margin Sales less variable costs.

Correlation The degree of relationship between variables, such as cost and volume. Correlation analysis evaluates cause/effect relationships. It looks consistently at how the value of one variable changes when the value of the other is changed. An example is the effect of advertising on sales.

Cost-Volume-Profit (CVP) The dollar impact a change in production volume has on costs and profit.

Current income Income received on a periodic basis, including interest, dividends, and rent.

Economic order quantity The optimum amount to order each time to minimize total inventory costs.

Elasticity The effect of a change in selling price on product demand.

Electronic Funds Transfer (EFT)   A number of systems that are electronically linked via a communications network. Funds may be automatically transferred by telephone, telex, terminal, or microcomputer.

Exponential smoothing   A weighted average of past data is used as the basis for an estimate. This mathematical technique gives the heaviest weight to more recent information and a smaller weight to observations in the more distant past.

Financial leverage   A measure of financial risk that arises from fixed financial costs.

Financial model   A system of mathematical equations, logic, and data that describes the relationship among financial and operating variables.

Flexible budget   A listing of budgeted figures at different capacity levels.

Float   The time between the deposit of checks in a bank and their payment. Due to the time difference, many companies are able to "play the float," that is, to write checks against money not presently in the firm's bank account.

Holding period   The time period over which an investment is held.

Holding Period Return (HPR)   The total return earned from holding an investment for a stated time period.

Index number   A ratio of a current year amount to a base (typical) year amount.

Insolvency   A company's inability to pay debt.

Just-In-Time (JIT)   An inventory management system in which the company buys and manufactures in small quantities Just-In-Time for use, resulting in a minimization of inventory costs.

Lead time   The number of days between placing an order and receiving delivery.

Liquidity   Cash or assets readily convertible into cash.

Lockbox   A box in a U.S. Postal Service facility, used to facilitate collection of customer remittances. The use of a lockbox reduces processing float. The recipient's local bank collects from these boxes periodically during the day and deposits the funds in the appropriate corporate account.

Net monetary position   Monetary assets less monetary liabilities.

Operating cycle   The number of days from cash to inventory to accounts receivable to cash.

Operating leverage   A measure of operating risk that arises from fixed operating costs.

Payment draft   A draft given to the bank for collection, and then sent in turn to the issuer for acceptance. It allows for inspection of goods before payment.

Percentage of sales method   A financial forecasting tool involving estimating expenses for a future period as a percentage of the sales forecast.

Pre-Authorized Check (PAC)   A check written by the payee on the payor's account and deposited on the agreed date.

Pre-Authorized Debit (PAD)   Authorization given by the customer to the seller to routinely and automatically charge his or her account.

Profit margin   The ratio of net income to sales.

Raider   A company attempting to acquire the assets or the stock of a target company.

Recession   A downturn in the economy. Many economists speak of recession when there has been a decline in the gross national product for two consecutive quarters

Reorder point   The inventory level at which it is appropriate to replenish stock.

Residual income   Net income less the minimum return on total assets.

Restructuring   The rearrangement of a company's organization to reduce costs and improve efficiency.

Return on investment   The ratio of net profit after taxes divided by total assets (invested capital).

Risk   The chance of losing money.

Safety stock   The amount of extra units of inventory carried as protection against possible stockouts.

Segmental reporting   The presentation of financial information, such as profitability, by a major business segment, including the product, major customer, division, department, and responsibility centers within the department.

Segment margin   Contribution margin less direct (traceable) fixed costs.

Standard cost   A predetermined cost that serves as a target.

Standard deviation   A measure of the variability between actual and expected.

Static budget   The budgeted costs at one capacity level.

Sunk cost   A past cost that is not affected by a current or future decision.

Total Quality Management (TQM)   The use of high-quality materials, components, and labor in the manufacturing process.

Total leverage   A measure of total risk, referring to how earnings per share is affected by a change in sales. It equals the percentage change in earnings per share divided by the percentage change in sales. Total leverage at a given level of sales is the operating leverage multiplied by the financial leverage.

Transfer price   The price charged between divisions for an internal transfer of an assembled product or service.

Variance   The difference between actual and standard cost or revenue.

Venture capital   A financing source for new businesses or turn-around ventures that usually combine much risk with potential for high return.

Working capital   Current assets less current liabilities.

Index

ABOUT THE AUTHORS

JOEL G. SIEGEL is the author of 35 business books, including the bestselling *The Vest Pocket MBA*. He has consulted for such leading corporations as Citicorp, IT&T, and United Technologies, and is a professor of finance and accounting at the City University of New York.

JAE K. SHIM is a prominent financial consultant, co-author of the *The Vest Pocket MBA* and 32 business books. He is also a professor of finance and accounting at California State University, Long Beach.

DAVID MINARS is a professor of economics, accounting, and law at the City University of New York and the author of 10 books and numerous professional articles. Professor Minars currently practices law in New York City.